WONDERS OF GRACE

WONDERS OF GRACE

Original testimonies of
converts during
Spurgeon's early years

Compiled by Hannah Wyncoll

THE WAKEMAN TRUST, LONDON

Wonders of Grace
© Wakeman Trust, 2016
Compiled by Hannah Wyncoll

THE WAKEMAN TRUST
(Wakeman Trust is a UK Registered Charity)

UK Registered Office
38 Walcot Square
London SE11 4TZ

USA Office
300 Artino Drive
Oberlin, OH 44074-1263

Web site: www.wakemantrust.org

ISBN 978 1 908919 74 8

Cover design by Andrew Owen
Picture of Metropolitan Tabernacle eight years after Spurgeon's death –
Courtesy: London Metropolitan Archives, City of London

Printed by Stephens & George, Merthyr Tydfil, UK

Contents

Themes in this Collection   7

Testimonies:

The New Park Street Years
1854-61   17

Tabernacle Early Years
1861-64   59

'I would propose
that the subject of the ministry in this house,
as long as this platform shall stand, and as long as this
house shall be frequented by worshippers, shall be the person of
JESUS CHRIST – who is the sum and substance of the Gospel –
who is in himself all theology, the incarnation of every precious
truth, the all-glorious personal embodiment
of the Way, the Truth, and the Life.'

C H Spurgeon, preaching his first sermon in the newly opened
Tabernacle, 25th March, 1861

These reports have been gently edited in places mostly to
modernise punctuation and clarify abbreviations.
Where the writer has underlined text for emphasis, we have
used italics. Comments by C H Spurgeon in the margins have
been added at the end of the elder's report.

Over 1,000 of these reports were painstakingly transcribed
by Mrs Rachel Linkens, a member of the Tabernacle, who also
helped gather information and traced the numerous
sermons referred to in the testimonies.

Themes in this Collection

IN THE METROPOLITAN TABERNACLE archives there are more than thirty large volumes of testimonies of those converted during C H Spurgeon's ministry, 15,000 entries beautifully handwritten by the interviewing elders of the church. These are conversion accounts of men and women, young and old, living in Victorian London. These accounts contain fascinating glimpses of life in those times. Occupations include many working people such as servants, crossing sweepers, hatters, bookbinders, coopers in the docks, tailors, and candle and pottery factory workers. Health issues such as diphtheria and consumption are mentioned, and also social problems including alcoholism, domestic violence and illiteracy.

Many of those interviewed were

Records of Lord's Supper attendance of members were kept in the church registers. Above is the entry for C H Spurgeon. He has commented by his entry – 'a poor sinner'.

previously atheists, some with long-neglected Sunday School backgrounds, while others had been regular attenders of the state church out of habit and culture. Some were 'gentlemen' and well-off business people, many more were working or servant class, but all testify to the same change of life and new heart that conversion to Christ brings.

When Spurgeon became pastor, the church was declining and numbers were low,* but within a few years, thousands were attending. Spurgeon and his office bearers needed God-given wisdom and discernment as great numbers began to apply for baptism and church membership. It seems that not only had God prepared the young Spurgeon for a mighty task, but he had also prepared a group of aging office bearers to support their new pastor for the first wave of blessing.

On a weeknight evening each week church elders would see enquirers at the Tabernacle. For each one they would write an account of

---

* Spurgeon described the congregation at the first service at which he preached as 'a mere handful'. At the end of 1854 the membership was 313 (*History of the Church Meeting in the Metropolitan Tabernacle*, by C H Spurgeon, 1876).

their spiritual journey. Often the discernment they exercised can be seen in the advice given, and in further visits over weeks or months until they were sure that the enquirer was truly saved. The core of the testimony would need to show that the person was relying only on the blood of Christ for salvation. They would also be asked if they understood the need for the imputed righteousness of Christ. They would talk about the doctrines of grace and whether the would-be member was looking only to Christ rather than their own merit. If the applicant was not quite clear on some things, the elders might give further questions to be answered, Bible passages to be read and prayed over, or as one elder put it, he 'prescribed her some pills of precious promise with a little draught of sympathetic experience to wash them down'. They might be given the *Baptist Confession of Faith* to study, or be directed to attend one of the Bible classes to help them further. Many were very poor and had little education, some not being able to read.

The Sword and the Trowel of 1865 says that elders look for four things:

- Tenderness of conscience
- Attachment to the means of grace
- Desire to come out of the world
- Deep interest in the unconverted

If satisfied, an interviewing elder would give a card, with the number matching the report, for the enquirer to see C H Spurgeon (who from 1868 was assisted in this by James Spurgeon). A note has often been added by C H Spurgeon to these accounts.

The young C H Spurgeon preaching in the early years at New Park Street Chapel.

Spurgeon would spend several hours every Tuesday afternoon seeing many such people, taking a brief interval to compare notes with his elders. He would then appoint an elder or deacon to visit to ensure the applicant was living a consistent, godly life at home. Attendance at as many meetings as possible on Sundays and during the week was seen as a sign of true Christian life. Many were in service and had very little free time away from their work, but their new Christian instinct should be seen – to assemble together whenever possible.

Some were not accepted for various reasons, quite often the reason being self-satisfaction or self-righteousness. If the elders were satisfied with the visit and interview, the person was then proposed for membership.

This collection is a fraction of those from the early years when the congregation began its life in the new building, the Metropolitan Tabernacle. We include 40 from the earliest days in New Park Street

A note added by C H Spurgeon to one of the reports:– This poor sister came without her card for her husband had torn into pieces. She is a much persecuted, persevering and loving saint. She prays and *believes* for her husband. From her childhood brought up amid dissipation and sin. All her brothers and sisters remain in the world, she alone saved by distinguishing grace. May the Lord convert the husband. He will.

Chapel (when many services were held at the Royal Surrey Gardens Music Hall or Exeter Hall to accommodate the crowds). Of the 15,000 entries throughout Spurgeon's ministry, we have here reproduced just 138 as representative.

Many glorious themes shine through the books in their entirety, mentioned here to give the full flavour which cannot be entirely imparted in a small collection. The strength of these themes is very striking in the original volumes.

Preaching

Individual sermons used by God to stir spiritual life are often cited, converts quoting particular sermon titles or texts preached on as the initial means of conviction, and then referring to another, preached sometimes months later, being used of God to help them close with Christ. This is also the case with the printed sermons, with accounts of fellow-servants reading them to unsaved colleagues (who sometimes could not read). One report gives an account of a man working as a bookbinder, mocking the parcels of sermons he was binding until convicted by one sentence which seemed to loom larger than the others – 'Sinner, thou hast an immortal soul to save.' Spurgeon said evangelism and evangelistic preaching was 'the matter nearest my heart', and longed to see more soul-winners.[*]

Sunday Schools

Very many of the converts, though they had lapsed in church-going before hearing Spurgeon preach, had the seed sown early in life in Sunday Schools. Large numbers of unchurched youths were first brought into the Tabernacle through its large Sunday Schools. There are several instances where letters from Sunday School teachers have been used by the Lord to start conviction.

---

[*] 'Soul Saving Our One Great Business', a sermon in 1879 derived from *1 Corinthians 9.22* – Paul's reasons for making evangelism the highest priority.

In these early years the Sunday School at the Tabernacle had 900 scholars and 75 teachers. The Tabernacle also ran numerous other 'branch' Sunday Schools around London. By the end of Spurgeon's ministry there were 27 Sunday and Ragged Schools ministering to over 8,000 children with 612 teachers.

The biggest Bible class was run by Mrs Lavinia Bartlett whose name repeatedly appears in the testimonies. There were 700 older girls and working young women on her class roll, many being in domestic service and with little education. Illiteracy rates were high. A principal objective of the class was to help former Sunday School scholars. A report on Mrs Bartlett's class in *The Sword and the Trowel* of 1865 commented, 'The question has often been asked by Sabbath School teachers with painful anxiety, How shall we retain our senior scholars? How shall we prevent their going away from religious influences just when they most need them? They can be laid hold of by earnest and devoted teachers at that critical period.' However, many were referred into the class by interviewing elders.

Outreach and personal witness

The Tabernacle was a hive of activity with much evangelistic outreach undertaken by the members. Many distributed Bibles, tracts and sermons. Open-air and mission preaching brought in many (by the 1880s, very large numbers of Tabernacle members were preaching in outreach missions on Sunday evenings), and preaching

Note by elder Frederick Grose added to one of the testimonies:– I cannot help remarking how much good often attends a word spoken to our next door neighbours. How often do we hear from enquirers, 'I longed to have someone speak to me about my soul!'

also took place at homes of refuge. Women would make gloves and scarves for police and other groups, these being distributed by evangelists. Numerous testimonies mention the instrumentality of neighbours, friends, and colleagues speaking to them about spiritual things.

Gradual conversions

The majority of these conversion experiences are not instant, but start with a few weeks or even months of painful conviction and sorrow before trusting alone in Christ and finding full joy and assurance. One elder writes of one of the immediate conversions: 'although this case is one of those almost sudden conversions, still I feel quite satisfied.' Seekers often mention being greatly helped by the spiritual conversation of church members after services and the prayers of believers.

Worldliness and keeping the Sabbath Day

Another theme which shines out distinctly in the vast majority of records is the forsaking of worldliness at conversion. All is changed for the convert. Worldly pleasures are given up and the life devoted to Christ and his people from that time on. Pursuits such as the penny theatre, public houses, music parties, the use of popular songs, and gambling are spoken of repeatedly as holding no pleasure for the new believer. The markedly different life of believers is often mentioned as instrumental in bringing others to enquire into Christian things. The change was not limited to church attendance, but extended to all areas of life. One report says – 'She was deeply impressed *[by a sermon of Spurgeon]* with the sin and folly of singing the songs of Zion on the Sabbath and carnal songs in the week.'

The Sabbath Day is mentioned in numerous testimonies as a day now to be kept, with nothing except spiritual worship and service to inhabit its hours, although understanding was extended to servants.

The elders refer to the keeping of it as a mark of grace in the true convert. Sabbath breaking is cited in many of the testimonies as the subject of the first stirrings of conscience which brought them to seek the Lord.

Frequently testimonies state that converts will no longer be idle, read novels or newspapers, do gardening or go on excursions on Sundays, but rather be with the Lord's people worshipping and involved in service. The following is one of many similar quotations – 'No Sunday rides, no ballroom, no playhouse now, old things have passed away, all things have become new.'

Church of England

A number of the testimonies are of those who previously attended Anglican churches, mostly from mere formality, and had never before seen the need for salvation. In Victorian times most people attended their parish church at least on special occasions, and were christened, leading to complacency. They faced hostile opposition from families if they went to hear a dissenting preacher.

Prayer meetings and simple Gospel preaching

Finally, it would be wrong not to mention the part of prayer and prayer meetings at the Tabernacle. Numerous testimonies speak of relatives and friends who had prayed for the person. Spurgeon regarded the prayer meeting as – 'the most important meeting of the week. He often said that it was not surprising if churches did not prosper, when they regarded the prayer meeting as of so little value that one evening in the week was made to suffice for a feeble combination of service and prayer meeting.'*

Dr A T Pierson, who ministered at the Tabernacle throughout and after Spurgeon's last illness, commented – 'This Metropolitan Tabernacle is a house of prayer most emphatically…prayer is almost

* *C H Spurgeon's Autobiography*, Passmore and Alabaster, Vol IV, p81

ceaselessly going up. When one meeting is not in progress, another is…There are prayer meetings before preaching, and others after preaching…No marvel that Mr Spurgeon's preaching has been so blessed. He himself attributes it mainly to the prevailing prayers of his people.'

He also commented that the Tabernacle demonstrated 'the power of simple Gospel preaching backed by believing supplication…a standing protest against the secularising of the house of God by the attractions of worldly art and aestheticism. Here is nothing to divert the mind from the simplicity of worship and the Gospel…The Holy Spirit will not tolerate our idols. If we will have artistic and secular types of music, substituting unsanctified art for simple praise…we must not wonder if no shekinah fires burn in our sanctuaries.'

Where specific sermons are mentioned, we have (if the sermon was published) provided the title, sermon number, date and text so that readers can consult the originals. Information recorded by the elder such as the age of the enquirer and their situation – whether a servant, or their place of employment – has been included. Some of the comments added by Spurgeon to the testimonies have been photographed. Also included are annotations to explain references in the testimonies. Otherwise the testimonies are left to speak for themselves. They are of course fascinating from a social history perspective, but above all, the themes of saving grace, instrumentality of preaching, dramatic life-changing conversions, renouncing of worldliness, Sabbath-keeping and doctrinal understanding shine through.

HW

The Testimonies

The New Park Street Years

This first section is a selection of 40 from 1,200 testimonies in the Metropolitan Tabernacle church records from the first seven years of C H Spurgeon's ministry, before the congregation moved to the present site in 1861. (The total number of entries across his 38-year ministry is 15,000.)

> **Charles Stapely**
> 15 Russell Place,
> Bedford Row
> Age: 28

IS by trade a bricklayer. He never attended a place of worship regularly since he was a boy, generally spending his Sunday mornings lounging about the streets with some of his fellow workmen until the public houses were open, to one of which they would usually adjourn before they went home to dinner; the remainder of the day being spent in idleness.

One Sunday about six months ago, he had lounged about as usual until dinner time and then slept until tea time, but was quite at a loss what to do with the evening. At last he said to his wife, 'I think I'll just go and hear Mr Spurgeon.' He did do so, and determined to go again the next Sunday. On that occasion the subject of the sermon was 'The Divided Heart'. 'I felt that sermon,' said he, 'and from that time I longed to be a different man.'

He is deeply convinced of sin, though without a saving knowledge of Christ. He had come, he said, to be instructed. It was most pleasing to see the meek, childlike spirit he manifested and his emotion when told of the sufferings of Christ.

A card for Brother Hanks' class was given to him.

Thomas Moor

> **'A Divided Heart'** (276) preached Sunday September 25th 1859 at the Music Hall, Royal Surrey Gardens. 'Their heart is divided; now shall they be found faulty.' *(Hosea 10.2)*

> **Charles Francis Doyle**
> 24 King Street, Borough
> Age: 19

BELONGS to an ungodly family. About two years since went out of curiosity to the Surrey Gardens *[where services were held]*, but came away once or twice after hearing Mr S only to mock and 'jeer'. But could not keep away, and by degrees felt some interest in the services. The sermons began to rivet his attention, he saw himself 'painted' in them. His conscience was pricked. He was led to see what a sinner he had been, what ingratitude he had shown for all the Lord's goodness and for the great things Christ had done for poor sinners, and

Photograph shows an example of one of the many notes by Spurgeon written in the margin alongside the testimonies.

'Another wonder of grace. An aged father and a brother have pleaded for her all these years and here she is saved at last – CHS.'

that he would condescend to hear the cry of the penitent, and was encouraged to pray to him, and believes he has heard his prayers, and now he trusts alone in Jesus.

He has felt very anxious about his ungodly family, prays continually for them, and believes in answer to prayer the younger ones have been led to attend at the Surrey Music Hall, and is desirous to do something in the cause of Christ.

I believe him to be quite sincere but preferred that some of the elders should see him before giving a card.

John Ward

I agree with the above and am satisfied. *John Barrow*

Ellen Marian May
At Mr Baker's,
304 Ludgate Hill
Age: 16

ATTENDED a Church of England Sunday School until three years ago when she went to the situation *[as a domestic servant]* she at present holds. Here she remained in nature's darkness until nine months afterwards when our sister Elizabeth Farrow entered the same household, thus becoming her fellow servant. It appears that our sister was not long there without trying to do something for the glory of Christ and the good of souls, for she was made the instrument in awakening this young girl to a sense of her lost estate, and this too by relating the way in which she herself was brought to know the Lord.

The good work was carried on through the instrumentality of Mr Spurgeon's printed sermons, which our sister read to her. The result was great distress of mind which continued for three weeks, seeing no hope for herself. Her first view of Christ was in reading *Matthew 11* when she came to the verse, 'Come unto me, all ye that labour &c'. She felt that was spoken to her. Then was she enabled to look to Jesus and found peace in believing.

Ever since her awakening she has attended Rev Baptist Noel's ministry until November last, when a fresh domestic arrangement enabled her to attend New Park Street, where she greatly profits under Mr Spurgeon's ministry. And as she desires fully to carry out the command of Jesus *[to be baptised]*, gave her a card.

Thomas Moor

Note for visitor: Her mother lives 3 High Court, Old Bailey. She wishes to be seen there.

> **Francis Spriggs**
> 43 Alfred Road,
> Kennington Park

HAD a pious mother who now lives in Devonshire. As soon as out of parental control by coming to London, took up with wicked and ungodly companions, became fond of the theatre and ballroom and became a ringleader in vice. He and two of his companions resolved one Sabbath Day to go to hear Mr S when a sermon from the words 'Whosoever will let him come and take of the water of life freely' was by the Spirit of God applied to his heart. After the service was over he left his ungodly companions, went home and fell upon his knees in prayer being sorrowfully impressed on account of sin, and prayed the Lord would forgive him. He then opened the Bible and there found the passage 'though your sins be as scarlet they shall be as white as snow &c'. All this time he came without *[pleading]* a Mediator, and wondered his prayer was not heard for he was sure he was the person described, until at length light dawned in upon his soul.

> **'Come and Welcome'** (279) preached Sunday October 16th 1859 at the Music Hall, Royal Surrey Gardens. 'And the Spirit and the bride say, Come.' *(Revelation 22.17)*

He then pleaded the blood of Christ and while upon his knees this time he believes the Lord heard and answered him for ever since then he has become a changed man. The things he once hated he now loves and those he once loved he now hates. He feels very anxious for his soul's salvation. His only hope is in a crucified Saviour. Is also anxious for his fellow workmen and speaks to them as often as he can although subjected to great ridicule and contempt. Is anxious and willing to do something for Christ either in the Sabbath School

London Bridge in Spurgeon's time. This bridge (opened in 1831 to replace the previous 600-year-old bridge) was dismantled and taken by cargo ship to Arizona in 1967 to be used as a tourist attraction.

or wherever he can be useful. Knows the grace of God has kept him up to the present time and believes it will keep him until the end. It was with pleasure and also with gratitude to our Heavenly Father I gave this dear brother a card for Sunday. He is a brand plucked from the burning. His wife is coming forward next week.

William Mead

Elizabeth Cox
17 Sidney Terrace,
Sidney Square,
Commercial Road East

THIS young friend has heard our pastor with her sister about six months. Before that time she was fond of worldly amusements, but was impressed with a sense of sin under the ministry. Felt her lost condition and compelled to seek the Lord by prayer.

She needs much instruction, and is evidently trusting partly to her repentance and partly to Christ. We recommended her prayerfully to read suitable passages of Scripture, and to come again in a month's time. She seems very anxious, and we believe a work of grace is begun.

Henry Hanks & Thomas Moor

SUBSEQUENT ENTRY: I have seen this young person several times since. She attended Mrs Moor's class at my recommendation, and appears to have been much benefited by the instruction she received there. This evening again conversed with her, and being satisfied that she looks upon herself as a poor sinner and nothing at all and upon Jesus Christ as her all in all, I gave her a ticket to see Mr Spurgeon.

Thomas Moor

Note: she is excessively nervous and needs gentle enquiry.

John Charles Samuel

THIS man until eight months ago was an infidel and blasphemer, a tavern lounger, and mocker of religion and religious people; a hater of Baptists more than any other denomination, and of the people of New Park Street more than any other Baptist. No name seems to have been too bad either for them or their pastor.

He does not appear to have been favoured in his parentage, for his father was a confirmed gin drinker and died raving mad from its effects. His mother, who is still alive, is both a gin drinker and blasphemer, so also are his brother and sister. This is bad enough but not all, for he has a wife and six children whom he was making as much like himself as he possibly could. He never attended a place of worship for 26 years until about eight months ago, and this is the account he gives of the way he was first induced to attend and the result –

I have, said he, a friend who has been a regular attendant at New Park Street for three or four years, and, though an unconverted man, he is a great admirer of Mr Spurgeon and often speaks about him. We had been having a pint of pale ale together one Thursday when he began to talk a good deal about Mr Spurgeon, until holding my glass up and looking through the liquor that was in it, I said carelessly, 'Well, it's no use, I suppose I *must* go and hear him,' not intending to do so and not thinking any more about the remark.

A short time afterwards my friend said to me, 'Did you mean what you said just now?' 'Said what?' I answered, for I had forgotten it. 'Why, that you would go and hear Mr Spurgeon.' 'Oh well,' I said, 'I don't think it will do me any harm.' But I felt sorry that I had given the promise, and the idea of going to New Park Street in the evening made me uncomfortable all the afternoon.

A short time before the usual hour to leave off work, a job came in that required my immediate attention. At this I rejoiced, for here was a legitimate way to get off my engagement, but my friend asked how long the job would take. 'Quite an hour,' I answered. 'Well,' said he, 'if one can do it in an hour, two can do it in half an hour.' So he set to, and it was done in that time, leaving me, much to my sorrow, no excuse whatever for not keeping my promise. I started with him

Workers at Covent Garden Flower Market. From *Street Life in London* by John Thomson, published in 1876-7. (Courtesy: LSE Library)

to New Park Street, thinking as I was going along that if I could get an opportunity, I would give him the slip by running down some passage or bye place, but he seemed to suspect as much for he stuck close to me all the way there.

I went in. Service soon commenced, and I must say I greatly admired the form of worship and especially the exposition of Scripture before prayer. But I would not bend down my head in prayer as others did because I was not at all interested in it myself. This peculiar position differing from all others around me made me feel uncomfortable. I liked the sermon, and thought I would go and hear Mr Spurgeon again so, at the invitation of my friend, I went to the Music Hall the following Sunday. This made me desire to hear him again, but as I was ashamed to tell my friend this, I determined to go alone in the evening to New Park Street. I did go, but preferred going into the School room.

After I had sat a little while, I thought I would not stop and got up to go out, and as I got to the door, I said to myself, 'Well, I will just sit down behind this door and no one will see me.' I listened attentively to all. In the sermon Mr Spurgeon introduced a character he called Mr Slyboots – one who, he said, did not mind going to a Music Hall on a Sunday morning to hear a sermon, but was ashamed to be seen in chapel, or if he did come would slink in and sit down behind the door. I felt that was me, so determined to go more boldly next time, and my friend, who has a sitting, enabled me to get a seat. I can't explain it but somehow or other Mr Spurgeon in his preaching took a view of me altogether, coming home so closely and personally with his remarks.

The first Thursday after my determination to come more boldly (at least I think it was the first Thursday) I was rather late and stood in the aisle, the rest of the congregation being seated. Mr Spurgeon commenced his sermon and spoke very much about infidelity, exploring the infidel's motives, character and all concerning him. He looked at me a good deal as if he knew I was an infidel. I felt he was preaching only to me, and thinking that the fact of my standing when the others were sitting had something to do with it, I determined never to stand in the aisle again. So next Thursday, being late from work, I went in and sat in a pew, but it was just the same. He seemed to know the thoughts that were passing through my mind. The sermon was again for me.

Thus it was until that sermon from 'The ungodly are not so'. Mr Spurgeon said those words over several times during his discourse – 'the ungodly are not so'. I felt them deeply, *then* it was I trembled and wept, and a good many more besides me did the same. After this I became very miserable. My infidelity had all vanished. I was willing to believe all I had previously denied, but I thought – how can I force myself to believe simply because I want to believe? Then it was that the sermon on the barrel of meal greatly encouraged me. But I did not know the way of salvation to my comfort until I heard the sermon from the text, 'Before whom Christ is evidently set forth crucified among you', and on Christmas Day when Mr Spurgeon preached from the text, 'Unto us a son is given &c'. Having put the question to each of us – 'Has the Son been given to you?' I felt I could say *yes*! And since then I have gradually been getting more light and knowledge.

> **'The Chaff Driven Away'** (280) preached Sunday October 23rd 1859 at the Music Hall, Royal Surrey Gardens. 'The ungodly are not so: but are like the chaff which the wind driveth away.'
> *(Psalm 1.4)*
>
> **'The Inexhaustible Barrel'** (290) preached Sunday December 18th 1859 at Exeter Hall, Strand. 'And the barrel of meal wasted not, neither did the cruse of oil fail, according to the word of the Lord, which he spake by Elijah.'
> *(1 Kings 17.16)*
>
> **'A Christmas Question'** (291) preached Sunday December 25th 1859 at Exeter Hall, Strand. 'For unto us a child is born, unto us a son is given.'
> *(Isaiah 9.6)*

Thus ended his account of himself. Mr Spurgeon's *hard* thrusts had evidently been made *home* thrusts by the Holy Spirit. The word was as a hammer, blow followed blow. He struggled, writhed, rebelled, still blow followed blow, until he was fairly compelled to give in. Verily there is nothing too hard for the Lord. Let sovereign grace be exalted, world without end.

Thomas Moor

Note: I do apologise for making this report so long and will endeavour to avoid a like transgression in the future. *TM*

Not a bit too long! A most blessed case. *CHS*

> **William Husbands**
> of No 3 New Street,
> Battersea Fields
> Employed at Mr Burns,
> Borough Road Mills
> Age: 19

HIS brother has recently sought membership with us. Parents pious people, belonging to Price's Factory, Vauxhall.* Mother a decided Christian. Father simply moral before, but through conversations of his brother and himself, led to see the Gospel.

His first conviction of sin – used to buy a newspaper on Sunday to aggravate his parents who were over particular, as he thought, about the Sabbath. Was deeply affected in November 1857 by reading of a shipwreck in a Sunday newspaper – at that time a despiser of God and in the habit of attending a religious meeting to ridicule. After much sore trouble, brought into liberty by attending a private prayer meeting. Gives an interesting account of a Christian friend kneeling down with him and praying for him.

> **'A Faithful Friend'** (120) preached Sunday March 8th 1857 at the Music Hall, Royal Surrey Gardens. 'There is a friend that sticketh closer than a brother.' *(Proverbs 18.24)*

First heard Mr S at the Music Hall, 'A friend sticketh closer than a brother' the subject. Has found much profit both to his heart and his understanding from the ministry. Expresses himself clearly and feelingly about salvation by grace – forgiveness of sins and the witness of the Holy Spirit in his heart. Thinks that Christ died only

---

* Several testimonies in the archives mention Price's Candle Factory – see page 56 for background.

for his own people because his blood was too precious to be shed in vain. Feels baptism a bounden duty because a command of Jesus.

Gave him a card without hesitation. *B W Carr*

> **Ann Hobcroft**
> 25 Maltby Street,
> Bermondsey

HAS heard Mr Spurgeon about ten months with much profit. Had attended Sunday School and often heard the Word preached but thought nothing of it until the sermon, 'The bed is shorter than that a man can stretch himself on it,' which awakened her to see her hopeless state – she found as a sinner she had no bed long enough to stretch herself upon, was deeply concerned about her soul, went home that night to

The testimony on the left probably refers to the shipwreck of the *Catherine Adamson*. There were two shipwrecks within nine weeks of each other, both sailing from England to North Head, Sydney. The first of the two was the *Dunbar* in August 1857, one of the worst sea disasters in New South Wales with 121 people lost. This, together with the second wreck, the *Catherine Adamson*, after an 87-day journey from Falmouth, greatly increased the sense of danger of long-distance sea journeys and led to a lighthouse being built to guide ships to the Sydney harbour.

'The Wreck of the Dunbar' by Samuel T Gill,
Courtesy: Mitchell Library, State Library of New South Wales

pray and was a long time under conviction before she found peace with God through Jesus Christ. It was during prayer God manifested himself unto her. Says Christ died to save just such sinners as she was. Ascribes the work to God the Spirit. An entire change – all things have become new – no theatre now – no Sabbath breaking now, the people of God are her dearest companions, the house of God her sweetest resort. Is ridiculed by ungodly parents but trusting alone in Christ, endureth with patience. Prays much for her parents. She says she could give up all for Jesus. Doctrinal knowledge good. Gave her a card. *Mr Roe*

> **'The Bed and Its Covering'** (244) preached Sunday January 9th 1859 at New Park Street Chapel. 'For the bed is shorter than that a man can stretch himself on it: and the covering narrower than that he can wrap himself in it.' *(Isaiah 28.20)*

> **Mrs Emma Wiseman**
> Servant at
> 27a Grosvenor Place,
> Hyde Park
> A widow

A POOR soul under deep conviction, with light enough to perceive that she is a ruined sinner, fear the consequences, and say bitter things against herself. That is all at present.

First conviction under a funeral sermon at Colchester four years ago. Has heard Mr Spurgeon as often as she could get out on Sundays for the past four months. First heard his solemn appeal to those in the gallery at the ordinance. Never felt peace but thought the sermon on the Prodigal Son peculiarly adapted to her own case. Seeks membership of the church from motives of apprehension that unless she takes some decided step her convictions will wear away, never to return.

I felt much sympathy excited by her remarks – prescribed her some pills of precious promise, with a little draught of sympathetic experience to wash them down. *B W Carr*

SUBSEQUENT ENTRY: This friend has found much peace within the last month from a sentence in a sermon of our pastor's which was

'Christ has paid the last farthing of our debt to God if we believe in him.' This has given her great encouragement and has led her to trust in him.

She is much persecuted in her situation for her love to the Master and for her wishing to connect herself with our church, but is willing to bear and suffer all for his sake.

I was quite satisfied that the good work has been begun in her heart, and although she is still serving the Master with trembling, and only, as it were, feeling for him, I felt it a duty, considering her position and circumstances of trial and discouragement, to give her a card. May God be with her and teach her the way of truth more perfectly. *William Olney*

> **'The Prodigal's Return'** (176) preached Sunday February 7th 1858 at the Music Hall, Royal Surrey Gardens. 'But when he was yet a great way off, his father saw him, and had compassion, and ran, and fell on his neck, and kissed him.' *(Luke 15.20)*
>
> **'The Death of Christ'** (173) preached Sunday January 24th 1858 at the Music Hall, Royal Surrey Gardens. 'Yet it pleased the Lord to bruise him; he hath put him to grief: when thou shalt make his soul an offering for sin, he shall see his seed, he shall prolong his days, and the pleasure of the Lord shall prosper in his hand.' *(Isaiah 53.10)*

> **George Perkins**
> 27 Commercial Way, Lambeth

WAS induced by his wife to come and hear Mr S about three years ago. The chapel was so crowded she was obliged to leave but he stopped. Had hitherto been a blasphemer, swearer and drunkard, and had not been in any place of worship for five years. The text he cannot remember, but he stood condemned and felt his lost condition. He went home to pray for the first time. I asked him whether, being such a great sinner, he was not afraid to ask God for mercy. His answer was that Mr Spurgeon said that Christ shed his blood to save sinners, and he pleaded the blood of Christ. Continued in darkness for a few weeks, but still prayed and was enabled to look to the Cross and then found relief. Attributes this change to free and sovereign grace, looks to God for strength to endure unto the end. I recommended him to get the Confession of Faith and come again. He has attended the Saturday evening prayer meetings for twelve months.

Seen by Henry Hanks

SUBSEQUENT ENTRY: I have seen this case and, fully satisfied, gave a card. *Thomas Olney*

Daniel Meal
24 Broadwall, Blackfriars

THIS man is a crossing sweeper, and while staying in one of the lodging houses in the Mint about two and a half years ago, first felt himself to be a lost sinner from an address given by a working man on the text, 'What shall it profit a man if he gain the whole world and lose his own soul?' He afterwards found a Saviour in Christ the Lord through reading his Bible, and has received great benefit by attending a meeting at the house of Brother Holliday for the last twelve months. He also attends Brother

Victorian Crossing Sweepers

The streets of Victorian London were often filthy especially due to the prevalence of horse-drawn carriages. Crossing sweepers would therefore use their brooms to clear a path in front of affluent people, who would often give them a small amount of money in payment. It was a job sometimes carried out by elderly or disabled people, as in the testimony above, or children who were barely able to do the task. They were sometimes viewed as beggars or a nuisance, but those that worked on a regular junction were afforded a little more respect.

Phillips' meeting on the Sunday. After hearing a very satisfactory testimony we gave him a card. It is such cases as this which show the *riches* of God's grace. Here is a man, poor in pocket, poor in person, born with only one arm, a crossing sweeper by profession, with a wife and two children dependent on the money he takes at his crossing (averaging about 1/- per day), yet he is *rich* in grace, an heir of the kingdom. Not only having been found of the Lord, but receiving grace to glory in the God of his salvation, knowing what it is to have sweet fellowship with the Father and his Son Jesus Christ in the midst of the busy hum of London streets, often in prayer while standing with his broom under his arm. Living a life of faith in the Son of God, confident in this one thing, that the Lord is all sufficient and will never leave nor forsake him. Verily the base things of the world and things which are despised hath God chosen. To his name be all the glory.

Henry Hanks & Thomas Moor

Note: this brother's crossing is at Evans Corner, London Bridge (the stove slate makers). Those who read this report will perhaps remember him when going that way.

Amelia Shepherd
23 Pardew Row,
London Road

CAME first to hear Mr Spurgeon at the Surrey Music Hall last Christmas twelvemonth. Used to laugh and scoff at religion and was addicted to theatres and worldly pleasures, but feels now dead to them and only loves the Lord Jesus Christ, his people and the house of God. Has doubts and fears sometimes. Believes that when she first heard the Word, she hardened her heart against it from fear of her parents, who are averse to her making a profession of religion.

The sermons she used to hear were felt by her at the time but left no lasting impression. Felt very low spirited for some time but with occasional seasons of joy. On hearing the sermon of 'The Three Woes' felt very deeply her sinful state, but at the prayer meeting after the discourse, felt the prayers of the brethren much blessed to her, went home and prayed and has felt joy in believing ever since. Cannot live without prayer and that very frequent.

By the advice of Brother Ward, I recommended this young person to come again as her experience was scarcely quite so clear as I could wish. *Frederick Grose*

Mary Howell
8 Peckham Grove,
Camberwell
Age: 27

WENT to the Music Hall, heard Mr Spurgeon preach from the words 'Compel them to come in.' She could not describe her feelings, felt she was blind, lame, and halt. In his sermon he said, 'Go home and pray to God to break your bars of iron.' She did so and then began to read her Bible in earnest upon her knees. Opened the Bible at the chapter where Christ raised Lazarus from the dead. She thought if Jesus could

> **'Compel Them to Come In'**
> (227) preached Sunday December 5th 1858 at the Music Hall, Royal Surrey Gardens. 'Compel them to come in.' *(Luke 14.23)*
> This sermon is mentioned in many of the testimonies.

raise the dead, he could her. Felt she could only be saved through Christ. Her heart was broken and she has ever since sought the Saviour. Up to this time she could read newspapers on the Sunday, but now nothing but the Bible and sermons. Under the above sermon was brought to remember her sins from her youth; had never felt them before. I considered it a good case and gave her a card. *Thomas Phillips*

The young C H Spurgeon

> **John Fletcher**
> 17 Liverpool Street,
> Walworth Road

UNTIL July last had never been in the habit of attending a place of worship. Was induced by a sister from Scotland who wished to hear Mr Spurgeon to go to the Music Hall. The first sermon he heard was from the text, 'Thou art weighed in the balance and found wanting,' when a deep impression was made and produced melancholy feelings. Was fearful lest an opportunity for repentance would never be given, and remained very unhappy for two or three months. But the impressions wore off, and he says he was very hard to bring to his knees. He looked everywhere for comfort but the right places. But at last he was constrained to look only to Christ,

> **'The Scales of Judgement'**
> (257) preached Sunday June 12th 1859 at the Music Hall, Royal Surrey Gardens. 'TEKEL; Thou art weighed in the balances, and art found wanting.' *(Daniel 5.27)*

and now sincerely believes he has found mercy through the Saviour's blood and trusts alone in Jesus.

He is a miracle of grace and is an anxious enquirer after the truth. Feels that a great change and a happy one for him has been wrought in him. He has an earnest desire to do good to others and to lead them to seek a Saviour. Believes that baptism is for believers only, but there is not efficacy in it apart from conversion.

John Ward

SUBSEQUENT ENTRY: This case was seen by brothers Thomas Moor and Mead, and they were perfectly satisfied, and gave him a card. *JW*

> **Elizabeth Polley**
> 3 Union Place, Edward Street,
> Blackfriars Road
> Age: 17

HER mother is a member of Surrey Chapel, has attended Castle Yard Sunday School for thirteen years, and heard Mr Spurgeon six years ago on 'The blood of Jesus Christ cleanseth us from all sin,' and was on that occasion convinced of sin. Has been unhappy ever since. Could not pray but has laid awake night after night crying on account of her inability. Her religious privileges have given her a deep sense of sin. Last Sabbath morning, our pastor's prayer was much blessed to her soul and the hymns also, but the evening sermon gave her peace. The text was 'My sheep hear my voice &c'. Can say that she loves the Lord Jesus Christ because he first loved her. He is her only hope, and she knows that she shall hold on her way because of the promises.

This young sister is well instructed in the doctrines, and indeed the doctrine of election seems to have been a trouble to her till last Sabbath Day – the Lord the Holy Spirit enabled her to receive the truth of it and its love. She wishes to be baptised because she feels herself dead to the world and believing it to be a command of Christ.

Was very satisfied and gave a card.

Frederick Grose

For the encouragement of Sabbath School teachers, I would here mention how greatly the instruction of our sister Graves has been blessed to this young sister. And a letter, a most beautiful spiritual letter, written by a young brother in Christ of the name of Baker (who died a few months since) to her upon the subject of her separation from him at the Lord's Table was a great help to her. This agency of letter writing has more than once lately been seen to be used by the Lord. I therefore affixed this note.

Arthur Morgan
35 Valley Street,
Kingsland Road

THIS young man is an orphan. He is lodging at the house of one of the Plymouth Brethren. He is a painter to a glazier. About 19 months ago he was induced out of curiosity to come and hear our pastor. He came to the Music Hall and heard the sermon 'Come unto me all ye that are weary &c.' He had never felt a sense of sin before and had never prayed. But that morning he went home to pray and did so earnestly. He did not however find peace but was in considerable distress of mind for some time, about six months. He at last found peace from hearing our pastor again at the Music Hall but does not remember the text then. He says he was brought then wholly to trust in the Lord Jesus. He feels now what a precious Saviour Jesus is. He loves him with all his heart and wishes to live only for and with him. He now feels a constant desire to love Jesus more and more. Prayer and the reading of the Scriptures and the Sabbath is his delight now whereas once he cared for none of these things. He views baptism as a command binding on believers only.

I found him a well informed and intelligent young man, and that the work of grace has made considerable progress in his case. I gave him a card with pleasure and felt perfectly satisfied with him.

William Olney

Annie Pearce
42 Long Lane, Bermondsey

SISTER to Elizabeth Pearce. Has been brought up under truly pious parents (whom I knew personally), and consequently in the fear of the Lord. Has had from her infancy convictions of sin, but could not realise peace through the blood of Jesus till lately – now it is her only trust.

About a fortnight ago the text, 'Go thy way and sin no more' came forcibly to her mind. She prayed most earnestly, and found great joy and peace in believing afterwards. She has been in situations where she has been surrounded by worldly people, but could not enjoy their society nor mix with them in their amusements. Her brother-in-law, however, induced her some months ago to go to a place of public amusement where dancing was going on, but she felt very miserable and determined never again to do the like.

Depends wholly upon Christ as her Saviour. Feels every day more and more the sinfulness of her heart, and her consequent need of her Saviour. Has found much blessing under our pastor's ministry, whom she has heard at intervals ever since he first came. Has great enjoyment at being in prayer, though sorely troubled by Satan's injecting evil thoughts while in that exercise. Has never been christened, wishes to be baptised in obedience to her Lord's command. Gave a card, believing her to be very sincere.

Frederick Grose

Matilda Jones
17 Lorrimore Street,
Kennington Park
Age: 18

THIS young person has been for a long time a constant attendant on Mr Spurgeon's ministry, the result being a gradual awakening to a sense of her alienation from God yet without a consciousness of the way of reconciliation. On hearing a sermon preached at the Music Hall from the text, 'Whatsoever thy hand findeth to do &c', she was impressed with the fact that Christ alone was the Saviour of sinners, and that as she had been exhorted to give *something* to Christ, she thought she could not give him anything better than *herself,* which she professed to do in prayer that very day – thus falling into the error so common with anxious inquirers that they must *give* something instead

This testimony mentions that Matilda Jones' Sunday School teacher was Miss White. The photographs below show two teachers called Miss White in the Tabernacle Sunday School during Spurgeon's pastorate.

of *taking* all. However she got no peace by it but rather increased sorrow of heart, until she heard Mr Spurgeon preach at New Park Street Chapel from the text, 'Come now, let us reason together, saith the Lord &c'. *Then* she learned the preciousness of the blood of Christ and salvation thereby. Since then she has had peace and joy in believing, and trusts to the blood and righteousness of the dear Lord alone for present acceptance and final salvation.

Thomas Moor

P.S. She has been six or seven months in the Sabbath School under sister White.

Alexander John Hamilton
11 Fashion Street, Spitalfields
Age: 20

USED to frequent theatres and was very unsteady until about four years ago. Was going out for an excursion on the Lord's Day when a heavy shower of rain stopped him. Went instead to a Sabbath School with a ticket that he received at an evening school, and from there to St Matthew's Chapel, Pell St, where he heard a Mr Cuffy whose discourse was the means of awakening him to a sense of his sinful state before God. Was in distress of mind for about five weeks. His brother (who has since become a member here but is now in New Zealand) brought him to New Park Street one Sunday evening about three years ago, and there he found peace under the discourse but cannot remember the text.

Has been engaged in Sabbath School work. Rests wholly upon Christ, upon his blood and merits for salvation. Believes he was chosen in Christ before all worlds, and that he will hold his way through Christ that strengtheneth him. He felt much comforted by the sermon at Mr Stoudly's preached by our pastor, 'The conies are a feeble folk &c'. Wishes to be baptised to show his obedience.

I found this brother very intelligent, and I believe him to be a sincere follower of Jesus, gave him a card.

Frederick Grose

Rose Edwards
6 Thomas Street, Kennington

HAS attended at New Park Street and the Music Hall about seven or eight months. Was first impressed under the sermon 'The Shameful Sufferer'. She then saw the love of Christ as she never saw it before and went home to ask an interest in it. She says that sermon convinced her of the very great guilt of her sins and led her to cry for mercy and forgiveness. She now enjoys private prayer and reading the Bible. She finds she is living a new life, has new desires, and with her 'that old things have passed away, all things have become new'.

> **'The Shameful Sufferer'** (236) preached Sunday January 30th 1859 at the Music Hall, Royal Surrey Gardens. 'Who for the joy that was set before him endured the cross, despising the shame, and is set down at the right hand of the throne of God.'
> *(Hebrews 12.2)*

She has a good understanding of the doctrines of the Bible and rejoices very greatly in the ministry of the Word and the Sabbath Day. She wishes to be baptised and join the church out of love to Christ and obedience to his commands. I thought this a very clear and satisfactory case and gave a card with pleasure.

William Olney

James Boyce
8 West Street, Nelson Street,
Long Lane
Age: 29

THE Lord met with him about fourteen months ago. Up to that time he had not attended a place of worship for 18 years, except to be married. For said he: 'I hated churches, and chapels, and everybody that went to them.' All his spare time was spent at the public house, gambling, skittle-playing and sparring, for which pursuits he had a special liking, being often thus engaged until two o'clock in the morning, Sunday as well as other days.

One Sunday about fourteen months ago, he had been spending the day in his usual godless way, and towards evening went out to meet a friend at London Bridge. But being disappointed in doing so, he thought he would spend the evening at Canterbury Hall (a music and drinking saloon in Lambeth). But when he had got as far as the New Cut, he says his steps were arrested by some invisible power. He wanted to go the Hall but felt compelled to turn back. He then thought he would go again to London Bridge to see if his friend was there, and to make the walk shorter, he came down Grave Lane and along New Park Street. As he passed the Chapel, the people were coming out previous to the commencement of the ordinance of the Lord's Supper.

On seeing the people, he remembered that his sister (who is a member with us) had often asked him to go and hear Mr Spurgeon, so he thought he would go in. He did so, and saw the service to the end. It did not make any further impression at the time than to determine him to reform a little and not go so often to the public house. Having carried out his determination by not going on the Monday and Tuesday, he thought he might indulge himself on the Wednesday, so as usual he went to the skittle ground, and *there*, in the midst of his old associations and companions, the Lord met with him in power, showing him the iniquity of his past life at one terrible glance. He felt he should sink to the ground. He could neither drink nor play but hastened out as quickly as possible, and has never since been there nor to any such like place. From that time he became a constant attendant both weeknights and Sundays at New Park Street Chapel.

For two months he was in great distress and darkness, thinking his salvation depended upon his own works. But one night when on his knees in prayer, he saw for the first time that Jesus and his salvation was a free gift, and through grace he was enabled there and then to cast himself on Christ alone. He has since been gradually *[growing]* in knowledge, faith and peace. The only foundation of his hope being the blood, righteousness and intercession of our blessed Lord Jesus.

He is another of the many wonders of sovereign grace, another witness to the power of the Holy Spirit to subdue the rebellious, another testimony to the greatness of that love, which out of the black depths of fallen humanity bringeth forth those who, being made white in the blood of the Lamb, become pillars in the living temple of the living God.

Thomas Moor

P.S. For the last six months, he has attended Brother Hanks' class. Brother W Olney has seen him and approves of my giving him a card.

Charles Sandell
37 Neville Street, Vauxhall,
near the Gardens

HIS early life has been dissolute and depraved, regardless of God and the concerns of his soul. But being a fellow workman in the pottery of Doulton & Watts with Brother Flood, he persuaded him to go to the Music Hall to hear Mr S about twelve months since. He continued to attend without any apparent benefit, though was frequently made to weep under the sermon. But during the absence of Mr S on the Continent, heard Mr Radcliffe, and some observation he made relative to the awful condition of those who sat under a faithful ministry, such as the pastor of this church, and who joined the service, and went on in sin &c &c, was made the means of convincing him of sin.

After the service, he had some conversations with Mr Roe and one of the elders, who told him it was not his tears that could save him but believing in Jesus. The conversation was blessed to him, and he was enabled to trust his soul on Jesus. Now trusts alone for salvation on the blood and merits of Christ. He daily strives against sin, and believes that he who began the good work in his soul will carry it on. He feels deeply anxious about his unconverted relatives and sends Mr Spurgeon's sermons to Australia to his brother. Advised him to come and see me or the elders again.

John Ward

SUBSEQUENT ENTRY: Came again. Feels himself a sinner, but since

INTERVIEWING ELDERS

As previously mentioned, when Spurgeon began the pastorate, the small band of office bearers were aging, but had clearly been prepared with discernment by the Lord to help him with the wave of blessing and the thousands of converts joining the church. We provide in these pages a few outlines of some of the early office bearers. They were men from all levels of society, but deeply wise in spiritual matters.

Thomas Olney

Thomas Olney was converted as a youth and joined the church in 1809 when it met at Carter Lane under Dr Rippon. He remained with the church through the changes, and welcomed Spurgeon. When he died in 1869 he had been a member for 60 years, a deacon for 31 and treasurer for fourteen. 'Father Olney' as he was affectionately known, was father to four sons, all church members. (His second son, William, was also the interviewing elder of many of the testimonies – see page 71 for information and photo of William.)

Spurgeon said of Thomas Olney – 'Never did a minister have a better deacon, nor a church a better servant…He was remarkable for his early and constant attendance at the prayer meeting and other week-day services. He had a childlike faith and a manly constancy. To believe in Jesus, and to work for him were the very life of his new and better nature…The poor, and especially the poor of the church, always found in him sincere sympathy and help.' And at another time – 'He never acted as a drag to the wheels, or a dead weight to the chariot. His purse was ready, and his heart and energy forced him with it to the front of the battle. In our great works of building the Tabernacle, the College, Orphanage, Almshouses, he never lagged or so much as thought of holding back.'

he has been in the habit of attending the ministry of Mr Spurgeon, he has been led to feel himself a new creature. Old things are passed away and all things are become new. Attends Brother Hanks' Bible class with profit, and declares that as he was once blind now he sees. Wishes to be baptised because it is commanded, and as he is a believer he felt he ought to be baptised. I believe it a genuine good case. Gave a card.

James Low

> **William Addington**
> No 1 Smith's Buildings,
> Bunhill Row

HAS attended Mr Spurgeon's ministry for three years. The sermon on the 'Shaking of the Mulberry Leaves' was made the means of his conversion. Ever since that time, the strife of the Spirit against the flesh and the flesh against the Spirit has been going on. The evening that he heard that sermon, he poured out his soul on Southwark Bridge, being a quiet spot, and God heard his prayer, and many times since he has found that a hallowed spot.

> **'The Sound in the Mulberry Leaves'** (147) preached Sunday May 31st 1857 at New Park Street Chapel. 'When thou hearest the sound of a going in the tops of the mulberry trees, that then thou shalt bestir thyself: for then shall the Lord go out before thee, to smite the host of the Philistines.'
> *(2 Samuel 5.24)*

Has such a sense of the wickedness of the heart that he is much cast down, but the sermon on Sunday evening decided him in coming forward. He could not stay away from the Lord's people, he must have a flag raised for the Saviour, 'if it's ever such a ragged one'. He long resisted the Spirit. For a short time after his conviction of sin, he tried to get away from it and stifle convictions, but he could get no peace. Now his whole desire is to love and serve the Lord, and prays that he would keep him in the right way.

I believe this to be a brand plucked from the burning, and have no doubt of the genuineness of the case. Gave a card.

John Ward

> **George Warne**
> 2 Suffolk Place,
> Batemans Row, Shoreditch
> Age: 58

I FIRST became acquainted with this man about three months ago, on being requested to visit him at his home by one of our sisters who, having some slight knowledge of him, stated that he was in a despairing state of mind. It appears that the whole of his past life has been spent in open rebellion against God and in the manifestation of intense hatred for everything good, being in very truth exceeding mad against the religion of Jesus Christ.

About 17 years ago, he was convinced of his sinfulness, and became very uneasy in consequence. But those convictions soon passed away, and he became, according to his own admission, more vile and demon-like than ever. He was a fearful swearer and would, even on a Sabbath Day, so exhaust himself with passion and swearing that he has, as he says, literally sworn himself to sleep, *wearied out with cursing God*. He has several times for a month together left his wife, who is a God-fearing woman, and when at home he has all but murdered her for her love of religion and religious duties.

Being determined, if possible, to make her give up praying and taking her children to Chapel, he has on their return from the house of God on the Sabbath evening locked them out, refusing to let them come into the house, and they have often been obliged to walk the street, all night sometimes, in the pouring rain. Finding this did not prevent her attending, he has burnt her clothes, but being an industrious woman she, by her own labour, procured others and went with her children as usual. These means failing, he tried what beating could do, and she has frequently been confined to her bed for days from the severity of his ill usage. He tells me he has often wished the Chapel would fall down upon them and crush them all.

Such was the character of this man up to Sunday, January 15th 1860. On that day his son-in-law visited him and stated that his foreman had told him to go and hear Mr Spurgeon preach at Exeter Hall. His son-in-law did not know the way to the Hall, and as he had nothing to do, he thought he would show him and walk to the Hall with him. He did so, and entered the Hall not thinking what he was about. The subject that morning was 'The Home Question' and the text from *2 Chronicles 28.10* – 'Are there not with you, even with you, sins against the Lord your God?'

'Ah sir,' said he, 'That *was* a home question to me. It went right into me, piercing me through. I felt there *were* sins with me, and *great* sins too. I came away greatly troubled in my mind and soon got into a terrible state of distress. For nights I have laid upon my bed trembling all night, the perspiration running off my body from fear. Sometimes I got a little ease by prayer but only for a short time, my fear and trembling would return again and again. In despair I have often been very near giving up all idea of seeking peace. Now I felt I could never read the Bible enough nor pray enough. I felt driven to prayer but it seemed as if I couldn't pray. Still, try I must, though I thought my prayers were only taking God's name in vain. I often wished the Lord would strike me dead rather than I should go on sinning as I had done. I have got great help from the preaching of Mr Spurgeon, indeed I couldn't get help or comfort from anybody else, but I haven't got full yet sir, I haven't got to the full.' (Meaning full deliverance.)

> **'A Home Question'** (294) preached Sunday January 15th 1860 at Exeter Hall, Strand. 'But are there not with you, even with you, sins against the Lord your God?' *(2 Chronicles 28.10)*

This was about all he said to me on this occasion and I left him, giving him such counsel as I thought needful.

Two days afterward he called me at my house, and as soon as he saw me he seized hold of my hand and said, 'I've found him now, sir, I've found him now.' 'Found who?' I said. 'Found *Jesus*,' he answered. 'I've come to the full now. I can say he is my Saviour, the load has all gone now.' The poor fellow, with many tears, related some more of his inward struggles, and also how he found a Saviour in Christ, a relation of which would make this report much longer than necessary, being already, I fear, too long. However from that interview I believe he had indeed been brought to trust in the one great sacrifice for sin, but would not give him a card until I had seen him again.

This evening, July 11, he came to the vestry at my request. Nearly three months had elapsed since I had last conversed with him, and upon my asking him how things went on with him, he said, 'Well sir, for a whole month I was full of joy, and then doubts and fears would sometimes arise, but Christ always removes them, and I know he is my Saviour.'

And so this man, who once hated all that was good, now loves what he once hated. Now he delights in prayer and reading the Word of God, and although he has burned his wife's clothes and beaten her to prevent her going to the house of God, he states that if the distance to New Park Street Chapel was ten miles there and ten miles back he would gladly walk it rather than stay away.

My heart rejoices to record how sovereign grace and infinite love has plucked this brand from the burning.

Thomas Moor

Mary Ann Warne
2 Suffolk Place,
Batemans Row, Shoreditch
Age: 43

SHE is the wife of George Warne whose case is recorded on the previous page. She was convinced of sin about 24 years ago and remained in darkness for two years, when it pleased the Lord to show himself to her as her Saviour. Since which time Christ has been her soul's hope for eternal life, and her soul's comfort in the midst of trials, compared with which the martyr's stake would have been a mercy. To see her husband brought at last to the foot of the cross, she considers does more than repay all that she has endured, and she can glorify God in that the prayers of 24 years are at last answered.

Thomas Moor

> **Elizabeth Powell**
> 111 New Dorset Place,
> Clapham Road
> Age: 17

SHE has been a member of the Wesleyan Body for the last three years and had no desire to leave them until two months ago, since which time she has constantly attended the ministry of Mr Spurgeon, and has thereby become convinced of the necessity of believer's baptism. She seems to have profited in every way under the preaching of Mr Spurgeon. Clouds and darkness have been dissipated, spiritual life revived, faith brightened, graces strengthened, and Jesus made more and more precious.

This sister manifests

   – much intelligence in her answers,
   – clearness in her views,
   – correctness in her doctrines,
   – and depth of feeling when speaking of Jesus.

Thomas Moor, Henry Hanks

> **William Avery**
> 17 Union Square,
> Union Road

ABOUT three months before Christmas felt convictions of sin under a sermon but cannot remember the text, but each sermon afterwards made deep impressions upon him. Used to go to church and has been in our Sunday School eleven-and-a-half years, but could frequent penny theatres &c on weekdays. The death of an aunt some seven months ago made him think seriously of his state as a sinner before God, felt what a great sinner he was, and the thought drove him to pray and he prays more and more. I could not discover that this youth had really found the Lord. I believe him to be a sincere seeker and should wish him to join our Brother Hanks' class,* if he can be spared from his school duties. *Frederick Grose*

---

* Mr Hanks' catechumen class was inaugurated for the study of the *Westminster Shorter Catechism* and was attended by many young men; it was one of a number of classes that developed for different groups.

SUBSEQUENT ENTRY: I have seen the above, my heart yearns over him. The arrows of the almighty are drinking up his spirit. God means to do something with that youth. He is ploughing deep, he hath not found peace, but I believe he is a vessel of mercy. Have given him a card to the catechumen class, and hope soon to see him rejoicing. *John Barrow*

There are many marginal notes added by Spurgeon alongside the testimonies. Above and elsewhere in the book are photographs of a few.

Mr James Thomas
32 Salisbury Place,
Walworth New Town

THIS young man is a nephew of our sister Mrs Winch. He has been under serious impressions for about four years. Was brought up in a Sunday School and had pious parents. Mother living and a member of an Independent Church at South Ockendon, Essex. Before he came to London used to attend a Wesleyan class. Has heard Mr S for fourteen months and was much opposed to the doctrines of free grace. He heard a sermon from our pastor from these words, 'According as he hath chosen us in him &c', which he strongly objected to, but was led to search the Scriptures for himself, which soon upset all his Wesleyan sentiments. And he was led by the ministry and prayer to embrace the doctrine of God the Father's sovereign choice of his people before the foundation of the world, and is now enabled to rejoice in the truth.

Declares his faith in the Lord Jesus, and trusts alone to his blood and righteousness for pardon and acceptance. Ascribes the change to the Holy Spirit. Wishes to be baptised in obedience to Christ's command. He has been in the catechumen class for several weeks, and I consider it a very satisfactory case.

Gave him a card.

Henry Hanks

Bertha Thorn
34 York Street, Lambeth

LIVES with our sister Nicholson but is employed at our brother and elder Jones. First felt convictions of sin from the watchnight service of 1857.* The solemnity of which so overpowered her that she does not remember any of the service, but

---

* The watchnight service was held at midnight on New Year's Eve, with prayers, hymns and exposition of the Scripture, 'that the New Year might be clothed with glory by the spread of the knowledge of Jesus'. This tradition is still carried on at the Tabernacle today, and hundreds gather in the lower hall for prayer and to hear testimonies, while the London fireworks display proceeds not far away.

was impressed with the idea of what a great gulf there was between her and Heaven. Thought before that she was as good as others, but was at this time brought to the footstool of mercy and to cry out for pardon, which the Lord graciously gave her a sense of on the very next Sabbath Day under the sermon, 'The Mighty Saviour'.

> **'The Mighty Saviour'** (111) preached on Sunday morning, January 4th 1857 at the Music Hall, Royal Surrey Gardens. 'Mighty to save.' *(Isaiah 63.1)*

Trusts for salvation on Christ alone, through his blood shed for her on Calvary. Loves prayer, hates the things she once loved. Wishes to be baptised because it is a command of the Lord. A very satisfactory case. Gave a card.

Frederick Grose

> **Emma Louisa Morgue**
> No 1 Dover Place,
> New Kent Road

THIS young woman is a daughter of ungodly parents, and she never remembers being taken by them to a place of worship but of her own inclination would sometimes go to a Sabbath School. She was very young when sent into service, where she soon became acquainted with another girl who led her into bad company and ultimately into sin. Too soon she found out her degraded position, afraid to return home, wandered about for six weeks but passing by Dunn's Lecture Hall, Newington on the occasion of a 'Midnight Meeting' breaking up, was spoken to by Brother Roe. Was afterwards induced to enter a cab and taken to the Southwark Home of Rescue Society, where the Word of God preached has been quick and powerful. And the 'once wanderer' says she is now 'being led into green pastures of God's eternal love'. Her great anxiety now is the salvation of the souls of her sisters in the Home and her parents.

She cannot remember any special sermon but gradually the love of God has been revealed to her. She has suffered much ridicule from her companions but takes her persecutors to God in prayer.

Her only hope is in the finished work of Jesus Christ.

This was a joyful evening *[of seeing enquirers]* indeed. *Three brands* plucked from the burning, by the grace of God, meeting each other to tell of his sovereign grace. With much pleasure gave a card.

Mr Roe

Emma Sofia Sutherland
5 Lower Rosamond Street,
Clerkenwell

'I WAS first impressed when aged three from the circumstance of a neighbour dying. I became restless and afraid of death. I resolved to attend church three times every Sabbath. At 16 I was confirmed. My father bought me *Pilgrim's Progress.* I read it with delight, and found at the foot of the Cross my burden dropped off. I always thought I must do something to be saved. At 18 I married my father's clerk, against the will of my parents. He pretended to be very religious but it was only put on. After I was married, he threw off the mask. My grief and suffering with him was very great. I have been separated from him two years last October. I have heard Mr Spurgeon six months. From his preaching I have been more enlightened. I see the way of salvation clearly. I feel joy and peace in believing. I have sweet fellowship with Jesus. I wish to be baptised and join the church.'

Think this a good case and gave her a card.

John Barrow

Alfred Catchpole
27 Upper Park Street,
Islington

'ABOUT three months since I became deeply impressed from my father's prayers. Up to this time, I had determined to have my fill of pleasure and went into it. I despised my father's evening prayers and longed for them to be over. But now I became impressed, I could not rest. I was afraid to pray and yet I could not help it. I knew if I then died I was lost. I sought mercy. I heard Mr Spurgeon from "The love of Christ constraineth us." I felt I could give myself wholly to him, then I could pray and trust in him with all my heart.'

This is a babe, but I believe he will become a man and a man in Christ. We must nurse him and give him the bread and he will thrive.

I have much pleasure in giving him a card to our pastor.

John Barrow

> **'Constraining Love'**
> (325) preached Sunday June 3rd 1860 at New Park Street Chapel. 'O love the Lord, all ye his saints.' *(Psalm 31.23)*

The father had best be consulted and the best time sought for the visitors to see him as he is not home until well after ten at night.

> **Mary Ann Mornings**
> 5 Cumberland Place, Old Kent Road

ABOUT two years since she had very deep affliction in the loss of two children and her husband. After this herself brought very low by typhoid fever. These were the means in the hands of the Lord of leading her to see her lost state as a sinner. She wanted to pray but could not. The verse:

> *'I can but perish if I go,*
> *I am resolved to try,'*

was much blessed to her. She read the sermon on 'The Smoking Flax' and this led to deliverance. She heard Mr S regularly until the calamity at the Music Hall, and she was there much injured internally and was confined to her bed for months, and her life despaired of, being given over by the doctors. I visited her several times, and she then resolved that if able to get up again, she would consecrate herself to the Lord in baptism. It is a good case. Gave her a card.

> **'Sweet Comfort for Feeble Saints'**
> (6) preached Sunday February 4th 1855 at New Park Street Chapel. 'A bruised reed shall he not break, and smoking flax shall he not quench, till he send forth judgment unto victory.' *(Matthew 12.20)*

George Moore

(Brother Frank has visited this case also several times.)

Exeter Hall, the Royal Surrey Gardens Music Hall and the 'Calamity'

When Spurgeon was first called as pastor in 1854, the church met at New Park Street Chapel, just south of the River Thames, by Southwark Bridge. The building was soon severely overcrowded and was enlarged, but still more room was urgently needed. It was decided to hold one of the Sunday services elsewhere to enable the crowds to attend, first, in the Exeter Hall, in the Strand. Then for three years from October 1856 services were held at the Royal Surrey Gardens Music Hall, with crowds of 10,000 attending. (When the Music Hall began opening the pleasure gardens and holding secular music concerts also on the Lord's Day, the church withdrew and returned to Exeter Hall.) Meanwhile, the church was planning for a new building – the Metropolitan Tabernacle – which opened in April 1861.

Readers will notice references in the testimonies to the 'Accident' or 'Calamity' at the Music Hall. This is representative of many more such testimonies in the archives referring to the terrible events of the first evening service there on October 19th 1856. It seems there was an orchestrated plot to disrupt proceedings, and voices shouted 'fire' which resulted in panic. Seven died and many were injured in the ensuing crush. This tragedy affected Spurgeon for the rest of his life, and the press vilified him, but the Lord brought good from it as many souls were saved after hearing of this event and going out of curiosity to hear the Gospel preached.

The Royal Surrey Gardens Music Hall

> **Martha Ellingham**
> 2 Short Street,
> New Cut

HER parents were neither of them pious. She lived in Clone, Suffolk and was in Sunday School where Mr Spurgeon's grandfather was pastor. She came up to London at 16 years of age, lived a worldly life. At 19 married a wicked man. Used sometimes to attend amongst the Wesleyans who urged her to the Lord's Table, at which she felt frightened. Curiosity led her to hear Mr Spurgeon at the Music Hall. She heard the sermon on the 'Faith of Rahab' which pleased her and induced her to continue coming. But the sermon on 'Surely I know it shall be well with them that fear God' was that which led her to see herself as a poor condemned sinner, and to cry to God for mercy. She feels Christ loves her and died to redeem her, and now she loves him.

> **'Rahab's Faith'** (119) preached Sunday March 1st 1857 at the Music Hall, Royal Surrey Gardens. 'By faith the harlot Rahab perished not with them that believed not, when she had received the spies with peace.'
> *(Hebrews 11.31)*
> **'Five Fears'** (148) preached Sunday August 23rd 1857 at the Music Hall, Royal Surrey Gardens. 'Yet surely I know that it shall be well with them that fear God, which fear before him.'
> *(Ecclesiastes 8.12)*

She appears to have a very feeble degree of divine light, but I trust she sees 'men as trees, walking' *[Mark 8.24]*. I recommended her to read daily and prayerfully the third chapter of *John's Gospel* and see me again.

George Moon

SUBSEQUENT ENTRY: Saw her again. Says she has read the third chapter of *John* and hopes that through the blood of Christ applied to her soul by the Holy Spirit she is born again. She came to the Monday evening prayer meeting in deep distress, but was much relieved by having one of the brethren pray for poor sinners, feeling she herself was the very sinner. Attends the Saturday evening prayer meeting. Felt very much under an address given there from the words 'examine yourself'. Gave her a card.

> **William May**
> 14 White Hart Street,
> Kennington

IS the son of Brother May. Was impressed from early age with sense of the need of religion and under those feelings used to attend the house of God on Sabbath Days, but having been induced to go to New Park Street to hear Mr S, the first sermon which was upon the 'Canopy of Heaven' made a great impression and induced him to attend the next Sabbath morning at the Music Hall which he thinks was 'A Call to the Unconverted' which produced the impression that up to that time all had been wrong, and indeed he had wasted his time, and went home very sad. Could not explain to anyone what he felt but was greatly exercised on account of the great sinfulness he discovered. He had

> **'A Call to the Unconverted'**
> (174) preached Sunday November 8th 1857 actually at New Park Street Chapel. 'For as many as are of the works of the law are under the curse: for it is written, Cursed is every one that continueth not in all things which are written in the book of the law to do them.'
> *(Galatians 3.10)*

been in the habit of deceiving his customers behind his employer's counter. But now he felt he could not pursue that course, felt great compunction of conscience for what he had done and would gladly have restored what he had wrongfully got of them. Believes that he is regenerated by the Spirit of God or he could never have looked to Christ. Trusts entirely to the blood of Christ for salvation.

I was much pleased with this young man. Believe him to be sincere and well informed having had a good religious training. Gave him a card. *J M Ward*

> **Harriet Elizabeth Bryant**
> No 4 Half Penny Alley,
> Jacob Street, Dockhead

HER husband is a hatter. She totally neglected attending public worship since she was married six years back – only been to church to be married and to have her little son christened. Her aunt and cousin have worshipped here a long time, and took her to the Polytechnic to see the dissolving views *[of the magic lantern]* and hear the explanations of the *Pilgrim's Progress*, which made a very deep impression on her mind and produced great alarm. This was twelve months back. After that her little son was taken ill, and she loved him much and feared he would die. For the first time she prayed earnestly to God to spare her child, and she believes her prayers were heard and answered. But she continued very unhappy under a deep sense of sin. By prayer and reading the Scriptures her mind has been greatly relieved and she is desirous of attending the ordinances to show her love to Christ. *James Low*

MARGINAL COMMENT: Must give this good woman a *Pilgrim's Progress*.

> **Susan Ing**
> 37 Tavistock Square

LOST her parents at the age of ten years. At the age of 18 came up to London, where she fell into all kinds of worldly pleasures and Sabbath breaking. Felt convictions at the same time that it was sinful but could not resist temptation. Now feels no pleasure save in the house of God. Was much blessed under the sermon entitled, 'The Mission of the Son of Man', also by an appeal made by our pastor after the ordinance to the spectators in the gallery, and felt especially comforted during prayer by the words 'Though your sins be as scarlet &c'. The sermon from the words, 'He shewed them his hands and his side' was also very precious to her. She is willing to give up all things rather than Christ. Though feeling daily the indwelling of sin, yet feels a sweet sense of forgiveness in Christ.

'The Mission of the Son of Man' (204) preached Sunday July 11th 1858 at the Music Hall, Royal Surrey Gardens. 'For the Son of man is come to seek and to save that which was lost.' *(Luke 19.10)*
'The Wounds of Jesus' (254) preached Sunday January 30th 1859 at New Park Street Chapel. 'He shewed them his hands and his feet.' *(Luke 24.40)*

Seen by Brother Barrow, who was well satisfied with this case and gave a card accordingly.

PRICE'S CANDLE FACTORY, VAUXHALL

Several testimonies are those of employees of Price's Candle Factory, Vauxhall. The son of the owner, James Wilson, an evangelical Christian and a pioneer of workers' welfare, provided all his boy employees with a Bible,

hymnbook and arithmetic text, as well as free breakfasts, suppers and baths. Services were held at the start of the day and boys were given 'school' lessons.

Pictures courtesy of Price's Candle Factory.

> **James Thomas**
> At Mr Pratt's, 183 High Street,
> Borough

THE first serious impressions which this young man received were about five years ago at Price's Candle Factory where a prayer meeting was held. His conscience there became alarmed for a time but this wore off. But his father, who is a Wesleyan, often conversed with him on the importance of seeking the Lord by prayer. This he did and was persuaded to attend the ministry here. He soon began to see his lost estate, great darkness and distress followed. He states he spent nearly a whole week in prayer for forgiveness. At last in the midst of his business, he was compelled to leave the shop and go down into the cellar, well nigh being driven to despair, and again prayed. And the Lord hearkened and heard him and delivered him, his burden rolled off, 'like Christian's', at a sight of the Cross, and is now trusting alone in Christ.

I have much pleasure in recommending this case, gave him a card.
Henry Hanks

> **William Lee**
> 4 Vine Place,
> Bond Street, Vauxhall

A STOVE keeper in Price's Candle Factory. Has attended our pastor's ministry for some time but although frequently convinced of sin, he never found pardon and peace in Christ till last Sunday. The morning sermon aroused him. He spent the afternoon in earnest prayer and the reading of God's Word, and on the evening of last Sunday whilst our pastor was preaching, he found peace in Christ. He says light came suddenly upon him and he saw the way of salvation by faith in Christ. A mist fell at once from his eyes and a new state of things all opened suddenly, and since then his faith and hope and joy have continued. He believes they will never fail, by God's grace and mercy.

He went home and told his wife all about it, and has begun family prayers and by God's grace he hopes now to live alone for God and his cause. He wishes to be baptised and to join the church to show his love to his Saviour. I felt very great pleasure in this case. It is a remarkable instance of God's presence in our midst last Sabbath Day. *William Olney*

Maria Culver
Borough Wheel Works,
29 Newington Causeway

THE attention of this young person was first arrested by a sermon of Mr Spurgeon delivered about eleven months ago from the text 'Come unto me all ye that labour &c.' Before that time she had never thought about coming to Christ, but when she heard that sermon her desire for salvation by the blood of Jesus was intense. For three weeks she was unable to hope but afterward through the instrumentality of several of Mr Spurgeon's sermons she received great encouragement and found peace in believing.

'The Meek and Lowly One'
(265) preached Sunday July 31st 1859 at the Music Hall, Royal Surrey Gardens. 'Come unto me, all ye that labour...'
(Matthew 11.28-30)

I have seen her several times, having at my first interview with her desired her to attend Mrs Bartlett's class where she appears to have received great good.

Having seen her again today I can now cordially recommend her as a babe in grace.

Thomas Moor

New Park Street Chapel. During the first seven years of Spurgeon's ministry the congregation's home was New Park Street Chapel, with many services being held at larger halls (Exeter Hall, the Strand, and the Music Hall at Royal Surrey Gardens) to accommodate the crowds.

Tabernacle Early Years

A selection of 98 from 1,700 testimonies in the church records from 1861-4, the first four years after moving into the new Metropolitan Tabernacle building. (The total number of entries during Spurgeon's 38-year ministry is 15,000.)

Charles William Pitts
20 Hatfield Place,
Cross Street, Blackfriars Road

THIS young man has been persuaded and encouraged to attend our pastor's ministry by our Brother Lawrence who works in the same shop. He first heard the Word at New Park Street but without any saving effect. He has attended regularly, and about three months ago a solemn appeal to the sinner, telling him 'that he had a soul to be saved or to be lost', arrested his attention and broke his heart. He was melted to tears and went home to pray for mercy through Christ. His past life of sin (for he has indulged in many) filled him with anguish for above a week, but through persevering in prayer and the conversation of our brother with him, the Spirit revealed Christ to him as the friend of sinners and peace and joy followed.

He is very inexperienced and illiterate but very sincere. He speaks much of the *conflict* of the *two natures* within. I believe him to be a humble believer in Christ and gave him a card.

Henry Hanks (Works at 52 Broadwall where he can be seen.)

Thomas Dugdale
85 West Smithfield
Williams, Coopers and Co.

WAS a member of the Church of England under Dr Dillon, but since his death has not joined any church, although he has attended worship. Last November he was invited by his sister to hear Mr Spurgeon, and the sermon 'The wicked shall be turned into hell' plainly showed to him that he had been building on a false foundation, that he had been saying 'peace, peace' where there was no peace, especially the second portion of the discourse concerning those who had 'forgotten God'. This cut up his morality root and branch, it threw him into great despondency. He felt a greater sinner in the sight of God in having so mocked him than ever a blasphemer would. He could get no comfort till one Sunday morning when our pastor preached from 'Come now let us reason &c'. Since that time he has felt his acceptance with God through the precious blood and merits of Christ. Wishes to be baptised in obedience to our Saviour's command.

A very good, intelligent and humble follower of Jesus. Gave a card.

Frederick Grose

William Allingham
A-2 Penton Place, Walworth
Age: 21

STATED that about two years ago, he was opposed to religion, but hearing of the accident at the Music Hall and being fond of fun and excitement thought he would go, in case there might be a similar reoccurrence. Mr Spurgeon's ministry caused him to attend regularly. The impression of the Sunday sermon never wore off till about Wednesday; he says he always felt miserable at the beginning of the week. When Mr S left the Music Hall, he attended nowhere regularly until the Tabernacle was opened. Has scarcely been absent since.

About six months ago he went to the Surrey Theatre to hear Mr Carter the Sweep *[evangelist]*. He there felt his lost condition. He pointed him to Jesus in his sermon but his state of mind was so dreadful for days, that all that knew him said he was going mad. He resolved to throw himself away if Jesus did not appear. Jesus did appear, and he found peace. Gave him a card.

   T R Phillips

Harriet Pitt
58 Cromer Street,
Grays Inn Road

I HAVE seen this young person two or three times, having at my first interview with her given her a ticket for the catechumen class as she had not a very clear view of the work of Christ for sinners. This evening I have again seen her and am more satisfied. She has a sister who is a member of Soho Chapel but a frequent hearer of Mr Spurgeon's. This sister brought her to Exeter Hall, and after attending a few Sundays she heard the sermon published under the title of 'The Wail of Risca'. Under this sermon she was fully aroused to a sense of her condition as a sinner before God, having previously been a giddy, worldly, prayerless young girl. She went home in great distress

The sermon mentioned in the above testimony was 'The Wailing of Risca' (349), Sunday December 9th 1860, preached at Exeter Hall, Strand. 'Suddenly are my tents spoiled, and my curtains in a moment' *(Jeremiah 4.20).* This

Courtesy: Llyfrgell Genedlaethol Cymru – The National Library of Wales

sermon was preached after a mining accident at Black Vein Colliery, Risca, South Wales which killed more than 140 men and boys. Spurgeon had previously visited the area for a 'delightful retreat', and had worshipped with the Welsh miners. The 32-arch long bridge across the valley at Risca was built in 1805.

of mind, relief from which she soon obtained by prayer for pardon through the blood of Jesus.

Thus far her testimony when I first saw her, but she was very confused in her ideas about the blood, and entirely ignorant about the imputed righteousness in which the believer stands complete before the Lord, and on several other points her knowledge was very deficient. I therefore gave her the necessary counsel and sent her, as before stated, to the catechumen class.

I am now however sufficiently satisfied and gave her a card.

Thomas Moor

Harriet Olney
140 High Street, Borough

HER earliest religious impressions were under the preaching of Mr Spurgeon when he commenced his ministry at New Park Street. These impressions did not produce any decided effect upon her outward deportment, sometimes she would be aroused to a sense of her danger and again, her naturally merry disposition prevailing, she would for a season be altogether indifferent. Two years ago she spoke to Brother William Olney about joining the church, but he was not satisfied with her testimony and could not therefore recommend Mr Spurgeon to see her. Though much disappointed, she now believes it to have been for the best as she has since then been more fully convinced of her sinfulness.

I have seen her twice and although her knowledge of divine truth is by no means extensive, she knows she is a sinner. She believes that Jesus died for sinners and died for *her*. She believes her sins are forgiven for Jesus' sake and that Jesus took her sins and died for them, and that she, by believing, receives his righteousness and for it will live in Heaven. She believes her prayers are unworthy of God's acceptance yet thinks they are accepted through the intercession of Jesus.

She is greatly troubled because of her many inconsistencies for, though Jesus is in the main most precious to her, she finds her heart often wandering from him, seeking pleasure elsewhere and forgetting him. This she grieves over and desires to know Jesus as her all in all, in every sense, and to love nothing as well as him.

Thomas Moor

Note – Her easily besetting sin seems to be a delight in the frivolous amusements of semi-religious society, such as music parties and conversational gatherings where Christ is either completely forgotten or conveniently put to one side for the evening. Although *all* Christians who encourage such things are alike inconsistent, yet their sad effects are in some more lamentably conspicuous than in others, and I believe to *her* they are so from her naturally lively disposition, her impulsive nature and peculiar mental organisation. If she does not crucify the flesh herein I much fear she will mar her testimony and her peace. She knows her weakness and fears, and says she is determined to seek grace to enable her to walk as becometh a follower of Jesus.

> **Charles Foster**
> 3 York Place, Put Street,
> Old Kent Road

THIS is an instance of the good results of 'compelling them to come in'. He was first induced to come by a man who has heard our pastor for years, and the very first night, the night after the fire broke out in Tooley Street, the Lord convinced him of sin. Before this, he was one of the worst characters, he says. There was scarcely a vice that he was not guilty of, but he has to bless God that he has been enabled by divine grace to overcome them. The sense of his sin drove him to prayer, and by degrees he obtained peace through the blood of Jesus. Last Sunday's sermon, 'The shield of faith', was much blessed to

> **'The Shield of Faith'**
> (416) preached Sunday October 27th 1861 at the Metropolitan Tabernacle. 'Above all, taking the shield of faith, wherewith ye shall be able to quench all the fiery darts of the wicked.'
> *(Ephesians 6.16)*

him. He can truly realise that 'old things have passed away, all things

The Tooley Street fire mentioned in this testimony began in a warehouse at Cotton's Wharf on June 22nd 1861. It raged for two days and took two weeks to bring under control. This incident led to the Metropolitan Fire Brigade Act of 1865. (Courtesy: London Metropolitan Archives, City of London)

have become new.' And that now the house and service of God is his delight. He enjoys much delight in prayer and reading the Word. Indeed for that short time he has been converted he seems to be well conversant with many parts of Scripture, although not much instructed in doctrines. Wishes to be baptised in obedience to the command of Christ.

This I believe to be a sincere follower of the Lord, and I gave a card accordingly. *Frederick Grose*

Sarah Ann Whitehead
3 Chatham Place,
New Bridge Street, Blackfriars

HEARD Mr Spurgeon for the first time at Maidstone. Was in the Sunday School there attached to the church under Mr Knott, whom she used to hear. For the last four years has heard our pastor very regularly. Had the advantage of a pious mother. *Cannot really say she is a Christian.* Knows that she is a sinner and that Christ came to save sinners, but cannot realise the witness of the Spirit within her spirit that she is born of God. Cannot feel that she loves God enough, neither feels sufficient sorrow for sin, experiences great joy under the Word at times – sometimes passes a *sleepless* night *feeling so happy.* This was the case last Monday and she *could* say then that she loved Jesus had she been asked, but now feels dead and cold. Her sister is a Christian, and her own tempers and conduct seems so different to her sister's that she cannot think that she is a follower of Christ.

I had a very long interview with this young sister. My impression is that she is a child of God but that the enemy takes advantage of a weakness of body (for she seems to me to be consumptive) and mutability of frames and feelings consequent thereon to suggest to her that she cannot be sincere, leading her to look to feelings and comparing herself with others, rather than looking simply to the blood and righteousness of Christ. I exhorted one of our sisters, who accompanied her, to watch over her and told her to make it a sincere matter of prayer to God to give her more settled peace and rest to her soul, and then to come again.

Frederick Grose

SUBSEQUENT ENTRY: I have again seen this young sister and was fully satisfied and gave a card. *Frederick Grose*

James Edward Hattam
15 Thornton Street,
Brixton Road

THIS brother heard our pastor for the first time when he preached the sermon on 'The Census', but did not realise any particular effect till the day the sermon was preached for the Baptist Mission. It was not so much the sermon as the prayer that went to his heart, made his eyes stream with tears; went home and fell on his knees in prayer. Felt his sins a fearful burden at this time, could not get peace for a long time, but now can say that he is delivered from the fear of death, which before was a great terror to him. He was a drunkard, a skittle-gambler and used to come home and swear at his wife, and often felt inclined to ill-use her in answer to her complaints. And now she is his chief stumbling block as far as the peaceable enjoyment of religion goes – sneering at him and telling how that he is going mad. His father was a professor of religion but walked very far off. His aunt however, with whom he was brought up, was a pious woman (doubtless her prayers have been heard for him). He can say he loves the Lord Jesus. Believes that his blood atoned for his sins. If left to himself feels that he should soon go back. He used to pray at night in secret, but a young man at a prayer meeting told him not to be ashamed of Jesus and now he prays aloud, much to the discomfort of his wife. This good brother is well known to our Brother Thomas Miller, both being postmen, who gives him a most excellent character as a Christian man. I believe this good brother to be a sincere follower of the Lord Jesus but untaught, being young in the way. *I have since thought it would be well if he could attend Brother Hanks' class, if he can conveniently do so,* but I only gave him a card to see our pastor.

Frederick Grose

> **'The Last Census'**
> (382) preached Sunday April 14th 1861 at the Metropolitan Tabernacle. 'The Lord shall count, when he writeth up the people, that this man was born there.' *(Psalm 87.6)*

> **Joseph Laker**
> 29 Smyrks Road,
> Old Kent Road

A BOOKBINDER. Was not attending any place of worship but rather opposed to religion. When a packet of sermons preached by our pastor was given him to bind, he opened the packet with the intent to ridicule, when some words caught his eye – 'Sinner, thou hast an immortal soul to save.' Says the words seemed three or four times larger than the others, and was deeply impressed with a sense of sin. Was induced to go and hear Mr Spurgeon. The first sermon was the 'Treasure of Grace'. Suffered much sorrow for about four months. Was nearly driven to despair, sometimes a little light, anon 'twas darkness still. Found peace in God through Jesus while engaged in prayer during one of his dinner hours. No concert room now, no playhouse, the Word of God his chief delight, the people of God his best companions. Wishes to be baptised to shew his love to Christ.

> **'The Treasure of Grace'**
> (295) preached Sunday January 22nd 1860 at Exeter Hall, Strand. 'The forgiveness of sins, according to the riches of his grace.' *(Ephesians 1.7)*

I was much pleased with this case and with pleasure gave him a card. *Mr Roe*

> **Edwin Dipple**
> 8 Ware Street,
> Kingsland Road

'OUT of curiosity' went to Exeter Hall to hear our pastor about twelve months ago being the first time for fourteen years. The sermon he says was, 'The Lost Man' or 'The man in trouble, he came to the hall of light'. But went away heavy loaded, with a sense of sin. He had to carry his load home when it thrust him down on his knees for the first time in fourteen years to pray. (O wonders of grace!) For a long time suffered sorrow on account of sin. Found out fresh companions who pointed him to Jesus. They wrote to him, prayed for him. Sometimes had hope and then again drowned in despair. The sermons sometimes lifted up and cast him down. But the sermon on 'Intercessory Prayer' gave him much comfort, and enabled him to decide for God. Is resting only on Jesus. Gave a card.

> **'Intercessory Prayer'**
> (404) preached Sunday August 11th 1861 at the Metropolitan Tabernacle. 'The Lord turned the captivity of Job, when he prayed for his friends.' *(Job 42.10)*

I was much impressed with his sorrow for sin, 'O that I could undo what I have done' seemed to come from fathomless depths and wring his very heart. I felt at that moment the elder and the enquirer were among the 'men wondered at' *[Zechariah 3.8]*.

Mr Roe

> **William Elvin**
> Private in Coldstream Guards
> R.A. 251
> Tower of London

WAS first induced to come to hear our dear pastor by a comrade and when he came, the Word came as a sword. He felt himself to be a great sinner before God and when he got home, he fell on his knees and earnestly prayed for mercy through Jesus Christ. And God heard and answered him, and his burden of sin was removed, and he rose from his knees a happy man. He found peace and believing from that very hour. Is very anxious to bring others to hear the Word of Life. Feels the love of Christ constraining him. Is very anxious to be baptised in obedience to the command of the Saviour.

Feeling assured that this is a wonderful instance of the sovereign grace of God and of his genuine conversion, gave him a card.

John Ward

This photograph is of an extract referring to the above testimony, taken from the 1861 Church Meeting book.

Lords Day September 29th 1861.

Our Brother Wm Elvin, having been previously baptized was this evening publicly received as a member in full communion with this Church. Our Brother is a soldier in the Coldstream guards which is about to be removed to Ireland, he was therefore received to night in the presence of many of his comrades, and after the public service, the pastor elders and deacons brake bread with him & three godly men of the regiment in token of the fellowship of the whole church with our Brother and in the hope that in that regiment the Lord Jesus may lift up a standard for his Son Jesus.

Confirmed.

C H Spurgeon

Oct. 2 - 1861

John Schott
17 Bedford Road,
Great Guildford Street

THIS young man when but a youth was turned out of doors by his stepfather (who was a drunkard) to seek his own living. He got among bad companions and was up and out all hours in the night, singing and rioting. Became a regular concert singer – used to sing burlesque songs concerning our pastor. After this he went to Birmingham from Bristol, his matinée place, and there was engaged about nine months on the stage. He, however, got out of employment, and his carefree companions all forsook him, and he seemed left alone in the world. One Sunday morning, however, he was led to hear a converted collier of the name of Walkiss. He had seen in his rambles about the town the bills advertising this service, and in his desolate misery he thought he would go. And he went, and Walkiss was led to speak of Heaven and for whom Heaven was prepared, in such a manner as quite pricked him to the heart. He could not refrain from shewing his emotions at which he felt much ashamed, he thought everybody was looking at him. He went home and prayed to God to forgive him. He was still in great trouble of soul. He was led to seek work in Bath, having turned a teetotaller and given up a young woman with whom he was keeping company but whom doubtless he felt was a snare to him in his earnest desire to seek the Lord. Here at Bath he heard a Mr Heartley, whose sermon upon 'The publican's prayer' gave him full release.

Mr Burton saw this case and was satisfied as well as myself, but is wishing to see Mr Spurgeon to tell him how he had 'travestied' him. I gave him a card. *Frederick Grose*

Jane Ryan
14 Well Walk, Hampstead
Age: 19

THIS young woman seems to have had her spiritual education neglected – her parents seldom taking her to a place of worship, but she went to Sunday School at times. Paid little or no attention to the advice given there and says she was always inclined to wander and disobedience, the recollection of which causes her much sorrow. At the age of 17 was led into sin by the enticement of a girl much older than herself. Afraid to return home, went towards Blackfriars Bridge, intending to destroy herself, but was stayed from that fearful act.

Away from home only six days, was rescued, and became an inmate of one of the Homes of Rescue Society under our sister Golding. Became much concerned about her soul by the religious services held there. Says one text by Brother Roe, 'There shall be weeping and gnashing of teeth,' was deeply impressed upon her mind. She had no rest but went about anxiously seeking Jesus. When one of the committee gave an address, he pointed her to Jesus and by faith she was enabled to behold him as her Saviour. Loves her Bible. Loves prayer. Father and mother are reconciled to her now. Is now in service at one of the members of this church. I was well satisfied, and gave a card. *Mr Roe*

James Melbourn
30 Little Bell Alley, Moorgate St

THIS good man wishes to join the church because his wife has applied for membership. He has frequently heard Mr Spurgeon and prefers his preaching to any he ever heard. I do not think he has the faintest idea of the Gospel. I suppose he is sober, honest, industrious and willing to join a church, or do anything else which is reputable and respectable. He reads parts of the Bible sometimes, and thinks it all very good, but knows no preference. Precepts seem to interest him more than promises. He never knew any answer to prayer, but attributes that to his never having prayed. He does not recollect having ever particularly prayed to God for anything in his life.

His conversation is extremely ingenuous. I am astonished how any man could sit under our pastor's ministry one Lord's Day, and be so entirely ignorant of his own ignorance of the Gospel.

I spoke to him of the new birth and gave him a ticket for Brother Hanks' class. *B W Carr*

INTERVIEWING ELDERS
William Olney

(One of the four sons of Thomas Olney Senior – see page 41.) In July 1890, just a few months before William Olney died, Spurgeon wrote in *The Sword and the Trowel*:

'We now give a portrait of the senior deacon of the Metropolitan Tabernacle, our friend and helper from the commencement of our ministry in London. Few men have such useful gifts, so precisely fitting him to discharge his office efficiently; and fewer still have his flaming zeal and persistent conse-cration, so as really to fulfil his calling to the utmost. Every member of the Tabernacle church knows Mr William Olney, and knows that in countless ways he is a faithful servant of the Lord among us. Great suffering he has sustained with amazing patience, and great service he has rendered with unflagging energy. He will soon be growing old; but no one would think it who observes his incessant activity…a ready speaker, a diligent visitor of the sick, and inces-

sant labourer for missions. Indeed, what is he not? Would that every pastor were privileged to have such a loving and willing brother at his right hand!'

At a service after his death, Spurgeon spoke on Olney's favourite expression in prayer – 'Living, Loving, Lasting Union' with Christ. He said 'I never knew a moment when he was not earnest. I never even knew him to be dull or depressed; he seemed to be always joyous and glad…When he was in agonies of suffering, and could only sit on the platform for a short time, there was never anything like depression about him. He was just as glad and happy as if he had been in perfect health. I wish that it were so with all of us.'

William Olney in younger years

Clara Rayment
11 Windsor Grove,
Coopers Road, Old Kent Road

THIS young sister, who is only of the age of fourteen, is a blessed instance of God's grace, both in calling her so early in life but especially of his divine teaching by his Holy Spirit. My first question to her was, 'What reason have you to believe you are a child of God?' She replied, 'Because I have the witness of the Spirit within me, showing me my own nothingness and sinfulness and the all-sufficient fulness of Jesus as my Saviour.' About 18 months ago she was taken very ill by reason of an attack of diphtheria. The doctor expressed his opinion that had it not been treated in time, she would have died. The thoughts of this strongly impressed her mind with thoughts of eternity – 'Where should she go were such an event to take place?' This question preyed upon her mind for weeks.

She prayed most earnestly, for she felt that she was a sinner and her consequent danger. She was praying one night with more than even her usual earnestness, using the words of Jacob, 'I will not let thee go except thou bless me,' when these words were applied with power to her heart – 'My peace I give you, not as the world giveth give I unto you &c.'

A few days after this she had a quarrel with her sister, which caused her such troubles of soul that she had weeks of darkness, night after night it seemed as though the enemy tempted her thus – 'A pretty child of God you are, to take offence at such a thing as that.' This continued till one Friday night she prayed earnestly that the Lord would show her whether she was really a child of God or not, and on the following Sunday she went into a little Baptist Chapel in Bermondsey Road and the minister Mr Chivers in his sermon – the text was, 'And the dragon was wroth with the woman' – so showed her all her experiences as those of a true child of God, that she knew that the Lord had answered her prayers and brought her again into liberty.

This is a most pleasing case. Her sensitivity manifested when I

Ellen Maria Underwood
8 Albert Terrace,
Royal Road

THIS young person has attended a Bible class for about six years at the Library, Lorrimore Square. Has heard our pastor regularly on Thursday evenings since the Tabernacle has been opened and very frequently on Sabbath evenings.

Her mother is much opposed to her coming and put many things in her way to prevent, if possible, her coming to hear there. But he who is for her is stronger than all they who are against her. She says she cannot stay away but must come to hear Mr Spurgeon whenever she can get out.

The sermon on Sabbath evening, 'He that believeth not', was the set time for her soul, and she by divine grace when she got home was enabled to write on her slip of paper 'saved'.* Samuel Pure is a teacher in the same school, she speaks of the deep interest he and his sister have taken for her soul's good. I was fully satisfied with her testimony and gave her a card.

W B Hackett

James Dow
No 1 Henry's Buildings,
Strand

FIRST came to hear Mr S at Exeter Hall about six years since, and has had deep convictions under the Word which seemed like a load about him, and has for all these years been carrying about with him an almost unsupportable load. Has frequently under the Word resolved to go home and unburden himself to his wife, but when he got home something within him seemed to restrain him. The fear of coming before the elders or deacons or speaking with Mr S was always before his eyes and seemed to shame him. All this time the Spirit was striving with him. He felt he could not stay away and yet he could not come, until about six weeks since when on his knees he earnestly

---

* Spurgeon sometimes encouraged people to write 'saved' or 'condemned' on a piece of paper at home, as in the sermon, 'A Revival Promise' (1151).

prayed to God to enable him to come and cast away his fears. And suddenly the weight was removed and he rejoiced in Jesus Christ, and felt he could keep it a secret no longer, and told his wife what he felt and enjoyed. And she said, why did he not tell her before, that was just how she had felt. And they both rejoiced and have ever since. He has given his heart to Christ and now wishes to make a visible

The Metropolitan Tabernacle, 1861

profession and obey the command of the Saviour. Gave him a card, feeling perfectly satisfied with the genuineness of his conversion.

John Ward

Mrs Dowsett
1 Victoria Place,
Surrey Square, Walworth

A HUMBLE but interesting young woman. The husband is one of our members who joined the church at New Park Street about 18 months ago. Her two sisters are likewise members with us. First serious impressions when she had a severe illness some months ago and was deeply convinced of her sin. Hopes for pardon by Christ but has no full confidence. She is a very diffident professor and a very unpresuming believer. Rejoices in the hymn 'Come and welcome, sinner, come'.

She generally reads the *Psalms* and the *Gospel of John* herself. Her husband reads Paul's epistles to her, but they seem too deep for her apprehension. What little she knows of the Gospel, she appears to have learnt in the school of an exercised heart. And she has found our pastor's ministry a great blessing. *Benjamin Wildon Carr*

A rather difficult case, requiring a diligent investigation. I think delay would be advisable.

C H Spurgeon

Peter Graham Pullman
29 Lewin Street,
Cripplegate

HE had pious parents whose influence preserved him from open vice when young, but leaving them to go to business, he plunged headlong into the sinful pleasures of the world and continued therein, never attending any place of worship until five years ago. About that time he was led by curiosity to hear Mr Spurgeon, and the sermon gave him so much pleasure that he determined to go again. It reminded him of the good old-fashioned doctrines that he used to hear when a boy. He went again and again, and then made up his mind to go regularly every Sunday, which he did for nine months. Going home as usual after service on the Lord's Day, he said to his wife, 'Well wife, it's no use. Either I must give up going, or else we must shut up the shop upon a Lord's Day.' He decided to shut up the shop and continue to attend. About three months afterwards, he was awakened to see what a lost sinner he was, and continued in great distress and darkness for six months, when he obtained deliverance and peace under the sermon from the text, 'I, even I am he that blotteth out &c'. From that time, he was able to see his interest in the blood of Christ, and through believing to find peace and joy.

P.S. He is well known to Brother Passfield.

Thomas Moor

> **Samuel Walker**
> 13 Chryssell Road,
> North Brixton

THIS brother has been a member at Lion St but was withdrawn from about eight years ago, having previously had quarrels and disagreements with several of the members. Since that time he has not been connected with any church but has attended the ministry of Mr Spurgeon almost ever since he became pastor at New Park Street. In doctrine and experience he seems to be sound, but I hope he has lost his quarrelsome disposition ere this, or he will not add to our comfort by being admitted among us.

Thomas Moor

> **Benjamin Hollick**
> 29 William Street,
> High Street, Lambeth

HAS lived until the last few months almost wholly regardless of the means of grace. Had gone very far into sin, been a great drunkard and a great blasphemer. After the Tabernacle was opened came once or twice to see the place and hear the preacher. Heard the sermon on 'How can I give thee up Ephraim &c'. The sight of the love and tenderness of God toward poor sinners melted his heart. Often thinks now it must have been a very sharp bolt that could break such a heart as his. Was brought into great anguish of mind. Went home to pray and read the Word, which he had never done before. Told his wife something of his state of mind and knelt down together and besought the Lord's mercy. Prayer seemed alone to give him relief from the anguish of his heart.

> **'Joseph and his Brethren'** (449) preached Sunday May 11th 1862 at the Metropolitan Tabernacle. 'And Joseph said unto his brethren, I am Joseph; doth my father yet live?' *(Genesis 45.3-5)*

For about a week found some comfort while in prayer, but did not lose the burden of his sin by looking by faith to Jesus until he heard our pastor preach the sermon on 'Joseph and his Brethren'. Is now resting alone on Jesus, and desires to be baptised in obedience to him. The testimony he gave was to me very pleasing and very satisfactory. I gave a card. He hopes his wife will soon come forward also.

William Perkins

> **William Cartwright** at Messrs W & E Hunt, 182 Shoreditch Porter

THIS young man is known to our Brother Spanswick who is engaged in the same house of business. He came to hear our pastor last April and continued to do so several times without profit. On one occasion our Brother Spanswick sought an opportunity of asking him whether he had ever thought of his soul's salvation. He acknowledged he had not, was urged to seek the Lord. He did so, and he soon discovered what a guilty sinner he was, and that God would be just in condemning him, but his only plea was the blood of Jesus. He gave his testimony with much simplicity and many tears. He felt that he was changed altogether. Bad company and bad language was hateful to him. Yet continued very unhappy until he heard the sermon 'It is finished' which set his soul at a happy liberty and he is now rejoicing in Christ as his portion. Wishes to join in obedience to our Lord's command. A good case. Gave him a card.

Henry Hanks

SOMETIMES SPURGEON OR AN ELDER ADDED A NOTE OF CAUTION BESIDE A TESTIMONY

Far left: I cannot see this case very clearly but I have hoped for the best. His story is a terrible muddle. It may be a skein of silk but I cannot unwind it. I trust the messenger will be very particular. He is out of situation and ought to get one. C.H.S. *[See pages 130-1 for full testimony.]*

Left: He has led a dissolute life since his pretended conversion 12 years ago – I do not think a man who lived without prayer can have been a Christian. He has, I think, been converted of late, but this case ought to be well sought out.

Opposite page: This man is in a muddle and seems to me to be rather loose in his head. This is perhaps the reason why he has not been promoted in the police service. I do not think he will be any great credit to us and should not be sorry if the messenger declines to recommend him. He has evidently overcome swearing and I think drunkenness, and it may turn out

---

James Bull
30 Robert Street,
Pitville Street

WAS first led to think seriously of his state as a sinner about twelve months since while listening to the singing of a hymn by some persons preaching in the street. Soon afterwards was induced by his employer to attend (with some of his fellow workmen) the house of God. He attended for some time at Spencer Place Chapel, afterwards came to hear our pastor at the Tabernacle, where he now comes regularly.

I think the Holy Spirit is leading him to seek earnestly for the Saviour, but his ideas are very confused and his knowledge imperfect. I advised him to spend all the time he could in prayerful study

that he is a simple, silly but genuine man, however I beg the messenger to make *very* diligent enquiry, for I fear he is weak in the head and not very sound in the heart. I cannot judge, *character* must decide. C.H.S.

Below: note added by Thomas Moor, elder – Mr Hackett tells me that this young person is very inconsistent in her life at home, very disobedient to her parents and very quarrelsome.

of the Word, and gave him a card to Mr Hanks' class, desiring him to see one of the elders again shortly.

William Perkins

SUBSEQUENT ENTRY: Saw this young man again, felt satisfied with his answers and his experience of the work of grace in his soul. Appears from his statement to be deep and lasting. He has a humbling view of himself and exalted views of Christ. He says he is deeply anxious to bring others under the sound of the Gospel. He tells me what I was grieved to hear that he *cannot read*, but his wife is teaching him to read and he says he is determined to learn. And this may in some measure account for the indifferent way he answers some questions, but I think he is a changed character and the work of grace is begun in his soul. Gave him a card.

Emma Tucker
2 Francis Street, Waterloo &
1 Vine St, York Road, Lambeth
Out at a laundry

THIS young woman has heard our pastor for three years, but about six months ago our pastor spoke very plainly against 'song singing' which she was in the habit of doing. She was deeply impressed with the sin and folly of singing the 'songs of Zion' on the Sabbath and carnal songs in the week, and she at once discontinued so doing, and began to seek the Lord earnestly for forgiveness through the blood of Christ. She believes her prayers have been answered, and now she feels happy enjoying the means of grace and profiting much under the Word. She is looking for all that she requires in Christ and strongly declares her faith in him. She states also that the change wrought in her must be of God's grace and nothing in herself. She is evidently weak and needs instruction and recommended her to our sister Bartlett's class. Gave her a card.

Henry Hanks

SUBSEQUENT ENTRY: Being dissatisfied with this friend, I referred her to Thomas Moor, but seeing her again after having been in Mrs Bartlett's class I was pleased with her.

Mary Ann Beverton
54 Devonshire Terrace,
Kennington Lane

THIS young person attended Sunday School, but says only trifled away her precious time, no care for her soul. Father died. She went to service where a kind fellow servant used to read to her. Was often seriously impressed, but the hearing of the sermon *[preached some years before]*, 'Paul's desire to depart' deeply concerned her. She says she felt

'Paul's Desire to Depart'
(274) preached Sunday September 11th 1859 at the Music Hall, Royal Surrey Gardens. 'Having a desire to depart, and to be with Christ; which is far better.' *(Philippians 1.23)*

she was not ready to depart which caused her much sorrow. Went upstairs to pray, and after some time light broke in upon her soul and she found peace in Jesus. Has been much tried but is still enabled to hold on. The promises come home to her at times, as 'Fear not', 'Lo it is I'. Sees baptism very clearly as a believer's duty and privilege. Her doctrinal knowledge on other points is somewhat weak, but I believe her a new creature in Christ Jesus. Gave a card. *Mr Roe*

> **Ann Hackett**
> Newick House, Carter Street,
> Walworth

THIS young friend is in Mrs Bartlett's class. I have had several interviews with her, finding she was lacking in doctrinal knowledge and had not very clear views of the way of salvation. I can now, however, recommend her to the attention of Mr Spurgeon. It seems she was awakened about twelve months ago but not through any special instrumentality. Up to Sunday November 1ˢᵗ she endeavoured to obtain comfort by her own works, but on that Sunday evening in the address Mr Spurgeon gave at the Table, he said to the spectators in the gallery, '*If any of you are not fit to join an imperfect church on earth, you are not fit to join a perfect one in Heaven.*' This alarmed her and as she says, 'I went home and cast myself on Jesus.' I am satisfied with the testimony she gives of the work of grace in her soul.

Thomas Moor

> **Emily Lewis**
> At Mrs Mason's,
> 33 Trinity Street, Borough

THIS young woman has been in our sister Mason's service for the last five years. It appears about two years ago she was dangerously ill and it was feared she would not recover. And her mistress as well as her medical attendant (a godly man) talked very seriously to her and prayed for her. After her recovery she was invited to attend the ministry of our pastor. This she refused, and her mistress lent her the sermon entitled, 'Compel them to come in', to read. This she refused until some time after. When she did read it, she was in great distress of mind. She felt herself a lost soul, and she began to pray and to seek for mercy through Christ. She opened her mind to her mistress, and she prayed for her and instructed her. And after a few weeks through the ministry of our pastor and prayer, peace was realised, and she has been enabled to believe in

> **'Compel Them to Come In'**
> (227) preached Sunday December 5th 1858 at the Music Hall, Royal Surrey Gardens. 'Compel them to come in.' *(Luke 14.23)*
> Readers will notice in this section of the book that the printed sermons were often instrumental years after being preached.

Christ to the salvation of her soul. Also a great change in her temper and general deportment was effected. A genuine case of repentance and faith. Gave her a card. *Henry Hanks*

> **Henry Archer**
> 18 Bowlings, Kennington

IS the son of ungodly parents who kept a public house. Was led into bad company by the young men who frequented his father's house in the evening. The playing house was his constant delight, even took money from his father to obtain

The Metropolitan Tabernacle eight years after Spurgeon's death
(Courtesy: London Metropolitan Archives, City of London)

admission to the theatre. In this downward career was arrested by Mr King who pointed out to him the sin and folly of his path. Was induced to attend a School at Lambeth in the evening. He still could not forsake the theatre. On one evening when going to the play, on his road these words came across his mind – Shall I go to the play or no? (These words flashed across his mind as rapidly as the former thought – 'Peace, peace, where there is no peace.') He at once resolved not to go to the play that evening. His feet were led that evening to the house of prayer. In the course of Mr Spurgeon's sermon he spoke of those who were seeking peace, where peace could never be found. He has become a teacher in a Ragged School. I believe him to be a sincere believer in Christ Jesus. *W B Hackett*

Eliza Russell
16 Crosby Row, Walworth

THIS friend is the wife of Charles Russell (now a candidate for baptism), and is very anxious to join the church with her husband. She has had a religious education but never thought seriously about her soul until the Tabernacle was opened. From that time she has been seeking the Lord by prayer and reading the Word.

Experienced great depression of spirits on account of sin, which was increased by hearing the sermon of our pastor on 'The Salvation of Infants', having lost one herself, and the remarks then made as to the 'awful condition of a parent being lost in hell, and her child saved'. Her heart was broken, and she went home in great earnestness to plead with the Lord for

'Infant Salvation'
(411) preached Sunday September 29th 1861 at the Metropolitan Tabernacle. 'Is it well with the child? And she answered, It is well.'
(2 Kings 4.26)

pardon through the blood of Christ. Her prayer was answered, and now peace came, and she is resting alone on the finished work of Christ. Her anxiety now is to follow the Lord with her husband in baptism. A satisfactory case, gave her a card. *Henry Hanks*

> **Joseph Ninian**
> 31 Alfred Road,
> Kennington Park

AROUSED under the last chol-era visitation, remained for eight years with a bleeding heart and found no balm. Heard me at Mr Rogers', and when I came out, I said, 'God bless you.' This cheered him. He found peace through W Olney's prayer at one of the opening prayer meetings. Has been a great play-goer. Is a plain, earnest, loving man. Says 'It is all of grace.' Been 20 years in present situation.

CHS

Mr Cornish being dead, this man was forgotten, hence these notes from my hand. This page and three following were left blank by our dear Brother Cornish, who has ascended to the seats of the elders before the throne. A notable instance of human mortality.

> **Emma Wilcox**
> 24 Borough Road, Southwark

THIS person has led a very thought-less life. Fond of the gaieties of the world. Theatres, concerts and driving out on Sundays, occupied a great part of her time. At last she was induced to come and hear our pastor through one of our members (Miss Alderman), and has attended more or less since the Tabernacle has been opened.

Many sermons have been blessed to her. Some causing much sorrow on account of sin, some to cheer her drooping spirits, but the 'Broken Column' enabled her to decide for Christ. Says a decided change has taken place. No Sunday rides, no ballroom, no play-house now, old things have passed away, all things have become new. Wishes to show her love to Jesus by meeting with his people and desires to be baptised.

> **'The Broken Column'**
> (403) preached Sunday August 4th 1861 at the Metropolitan Tabernacle. 'And another also said, Lord, I will follow thee; but...' (Luke 9.61)

Note: This person deeply grieves and mourns over her past life in that it should have been spent in the world. The Holy Spirit truly brings 'all things to her remembrance' and her cry is 'O the Sabbath days I have wasted.' She is much concerned about her relations and acquaintances. Her husband is a hearer of our pastor and I intend to call and see him. It was with much pleasure I gave her a card.

Mr Roe

> **Sarah Ann Betts**
> 10 High Street, Newington,
> opposite the church
> Age: 29

I HOPE this young person is really enquiring after the way of salvation, but as she has been so short a time as four months hearing Mr S, and her views of the Gospel plan of salvation are so feeble and obscure, I recommended her to continue hearing Mr S longer and to see me again. The poor thing wept much, and I felt much for her, and gave her Smith's tract on church communion. I shall look after her.

George Moon

> **James Kirkwood**
> 55 Hill St, Wellington Street,
> Blackfriars Road

I BELIEVE the Spirit's mighty work is evident in this man – convictions deep, tears many, prayers earnest and melting, peace groaningly sought for, and holy joy at last by believing in Christ. He does not believe in the election of grace. I therefore gave him a few hints on the subject and a card to Brother Hanks' class, and will see him again. *Thomas Moor*

NOTE BY MARGIN: Has been throughout Canada and United States. His father an old and carnal professor in Edinburgh and set him an ill example. The *reading* of my sermons long before he heard the word has been blessed to him. *CHS*

SUBSEQUENT ENTRY: I have seen him again this evening, and found that through a sermon of Mr Spurgeon's preached a fortnight after I saw him last and through the kind instruction of a friend of his, he has been led not only to see that the doctrine of election is a doctrine of the Bible, but to rejoice in that doctrine as one that exalts the wisdom and love of God. *Thomas Moor*

Benjamin Carrick
85 Great Bland Street,
Dover Road

WAS converted under the ministry of a Mr Blackman in Devonshire about fourteen years ago and was baptised. For about five years he walked consistently with his Christian profession, but at the termination of this time they were left without a minister and had supplies for about six months. These supplies were for the most part of the Hyper-Calvinistic school, and one especially who was an ultra Hyper preached him into downright antinomianism.

He led a careless life and fell into sin. About eight years ago he came to London and used to attend the house of God, but was very unhappy. At length in the good providence of the Lord he was led to hear our pastor, and the sermon upon the text, 'But the natural man receiveth not the things of the Spirit of God &c' seemed to give him great comfort. And he believes that he is fully restored to joy and peace through the blood of Jesus. He much enjoys the ministry of our pastor.

I believe this to be a sincere case and gave a card. *Frederick Grose*

'**Natural or Spiritual?**'
(407) preached Sunday September 1st 1861 at the Metropolitan Tabernacle. 'But the natural man receiveth not the things of the Spirit of God: for they are foolishness unto him: neither can he know them, because they are spiritually discerned.'
(1 Corinthians 2.14)

Jemima Lovitt
4 Trafalgar Road,
Old Kent Road

THIS young person was first brought to see her lost and ruined state by reading one of our pastor's sermons (Parable of the Sower) lent her by her pious mistress with whom she then resided at Highbury. In reading the sermon these words were specially blessed to her, 'Flee sinner, flee.' She at once thought of the reckless manner of her life – the theatre had been her delight whenever she could go – but from that time she has sought Christ and now rejoices in him alone. The Bible is her constant study and delight. Her knowledge is good, very clear on the doctrines of grace. Is desirous of being baptised.

> **'The Parable of the Sower'** (308) preached Sunday April 15th 1860 at Exeter Hall, the Strand. 'A sower went out to sow his seed: and as he sowed, some fell by the way side; and it was trodden down…' *(Luke 8.4-8)*

I was much impressed with her and gave her a card to see our pastor. *William Hackett*

May an elder of the church call on Mrs New *[her mistress]*, 4 Pannine Terrace, Highbury. It would be well. *CHS*

> **Sarah Ardener**
> 9 Prebend St, South Islington
> Her sister's residence

HAS been some years an attendant on the ministry of Mr Spurgeon, and for a long time under deep conviction of sin, from which she was not delivered until she heard the sermon from the text 'It is finished'. The Holy Spirit made the Word mighty – darkness fled – divine light entered, even Jesus the true light, and as a consequence joy and peace. *Thomas Moor*

Is in Mrs Bartlett's class and says she owes very much to her teaching. Cousin to Mistress Dottridge. She is an orphan, no religious training. Mistress Hill, one of our members, was living in the house with her and brought her here, as also two cousins who obtained

> **'It is Finished!'** (421) preached Sunday December 1st 1861 at the Metropolitan Tabernacle. 'When Jesus therefore had received the vinegar, he said, It is finished: and he bowed his head, and gave up the ghost.' *(John 19.30)*

peace *here* and have joined at Finsbury. She brings her dinner and so stays to the two services on Sunday.[*]

---

[*] This practice is still continued today at the Tabernacle with several hundred friends bringing their lunch and tea and eating in the lower halls. Many help with collecting and teaching children in the evangelistic Sunday School at 3pm. Tea is provided before the evening service for students and Bible classes.

Thomas Scott
13 Westmorland Street,
Pimlico

WAS brought up in attendance on the Church of England. Has for many years had seasons of deep anxiety on account of his soul. Has always led a moral life, but felt that something more was needed to save his soul. Had heard Mr Spurgeon regularly for eight or nine months (his wife has recently been added to our church). A sermon preached by our pastor in the Music Hall impressed him greatly, showing him the folly of depending on a form of godliness as he had hitherto done, and led him to seek to realise the power of it in his heart. This by the grace of God he has been enabled to do through faith in Jesus and can rejoice in his love shed abroad in his heart.

It is after much prayer and self-examination that he now offers himself for church fellowship.

Has carefully examined the book (Pengilly on baptism) and clearly sees baptism to be a command of the Saviour.

This is a very intelligent young man and I believe a *humble* follower of our Lord Jesus Christ. Gave him a card with much pleasure. *William Perkins*

Sarah Ingram
9 Eltham Street, Walworth

HAS felt religious impressions for the last 20 years, she believes. Her husband is very ungodly and she suffers *very* much from him. The death of a little child to whom she was devotedly attached was the means under God's blessing of making her think seriously of her eternal state. She was told that 'it had gone to Heaven' and the thought seemed to weigh upon her as to whether she would go there to meet it. She has felt much peace and joy in believing especially for the last three months, and profits much under the ministry of our pastor. She trusts only in Christ and believes that through his strength she shall hold on her way – even against all the opposition of her husband. She is a woman of many sorrows. She suffers from a cancer in her breast, and as she says 'has

Fleet Street, City of London: looking east to Ludgate Hill and St Paul's
Cathedral, 1890 (Courtesy: London Metropolitan Archives, City of London)

been brought through deep waters but the Lord has sustained her.'
Can say that she loves the Lord Jesus Christ and that all her hopes
are centred upon him.

This poor sister is truly an object of compassion. I had some
doubt about *her being able to go through the ordinance of baptism* as
the mere excitement of coming to see the elders seemed to make her
quite ill. I however gave her a card to see our pastor being satisfied
with her testimony. *Frederick Grose, J W Ward*

Alfred Denny
Windmill Place,
Clapham Common

THIS young man says that about
three years ago a brother of his
was brought to know the truth as it is
in Jesus by reading our dear pastor's
sermons. Afterwards the converted brother induced this, his younger
brother, to sometimes read them. Generally found something in

them toward the close which made him very anxious about his soul. Made him forsake his old companions and ways, led him to God's house hoping there to meet with a Saviour. Was led to pray but found after some time he was trusting to his prayers. Asked that the Lord would show him the way of life more fully.

Cannot say by what outward means but gradually he was brought to rest wholly on the Rock, Christ Jesus. Knows that his salvation is secure because he has believed on him.

I was well satisfied with the testimony he gave that the work was of the Holy Spirit. His doctrinal knowledge was good, his view of the atonement by Jesus Christ very scriptural and clear.

Gave a card.

William Perkins

I saw this young man one Sunday as I was walking home. I like him well. Mr Brown to urge him to bring his young friends to the district meetings. *CHS*

Alexander Hamilton
11 Fashion Street, Spitalfields

THIS friend is a cooper *[a maker of wooden barrels and casks]* in the London Dock Co. He was going out with some of his shopfellows about eight years ago on a Sabbath excursion on the water, but the weather being unfavourable he was induced to turn into the Sunday School belonging to the Dock Co. Went to the church service with the scholars. The sermon impressed him with a sense of his danger in the sight of God, and made him very wretched. But about five weeks after he found peace under a sermon from our pastor on the love of Christ. This gave him peace and joy such as he will never forget. Since then he has been seeking to grow in grace and to make himself useful in the Master's service by preaching in the streets and in Victoria Park. His views on Scripture, doctrine and baptism are correct and satisfactory.

William Olney

N.B. This young man has been proposed to the church for about twelve months, but through a mistake in his address I have not been able to find where he lived till lately. This is the cause of the delay. He has a brother in New Zealand who was formerly a member with us.

> **Ruth Gill**
> 34 Sloppers Place,
> Rotherhithe

THIS young person has lost by death a godly mother whose prayers she remembers, but they were slighted by her at the time. Attended the New Park Street Sunday School five years, but left for some time on account of her former teacher Miss Clark leaving. She again returned to the School, and dates her first impressions and convictions of sin from the earnest and personal prayers of Mrs Bartlett at the Bible class, New Park Street one afternoon some three months since.

For about three months was under deep convictions of sin and felt she must be lost. Found peace when praying at home in secret. After pleading for some time for mercy, the Lord revealed himself to her as her Saviour. Has some doubts and fear at times, but again finds peace through the blood of the Lord, and knows she is prepared to die because she believes and her sins are pardoned. Desires to be baptised to follow her Lord. This is a satisfactory case for Mrs Bartlett. Gave a card to see the pastor.

M B Collins

The father is piermaster at Cherry Gardens Pier. He will be the most easily seen. She works at Straker's Bookfoldcrs, Little Britain.

> **Mary Ann Sparrow**
> 127 Dover Road

USED to attend to St Peter's, Walworth in early life and was a teacher in the Sunday School there. Married and then ceased to attend anywhere except occasionally. Now and then heard Mr Moore of Camberwell, and still later now and then Mr Allen. In November last lost three children under four years of age in one week. Alarmed because they were not sprinkled, searched the Bible and found that there was no such ordinance.

These losses aroused her. Came here in February but is not able to say much of any one text. Found peace about a fortnight since while we sung 'Just as I am'. Her load removed and she is now rejoicing. Reads the Word, finds prayer precious, and knows that the change is more than man can work. Did sometimes attend theatres with her husband, but all this is over.

John Ward

> **Susan Avery**
> 17 Union Square,
> Horsemonger Lane

HOPES she is saved. The blood of Jesus Christ she knows cleanses from all sin those who believe. Has been in Miss Evans' class for eight or nine years. I could not by all the manoeuvring in my power get this young sister to answer my questions, and after I think nearly half an hour the above testimony was all that I could *drag out*, and I was forced to tell her to make it a matter of prayer and again come to see the elders. A fine opportunity for one of the elders to 'let patience have her perfect work'.

Frederick Grose

[See entry below for second interview.]

> **Susan Avery**
> Second entry

I GAVE this child a card to see Mr Spurgeon for, although young in years, I believe she is born again of the Holy Spirit. It appears from the account she gives of herself that at the commencement of the present year she went to Trinity Church to hear the New Year sermon, and the words, 'This year thou shalt die' greatly alarmed her. She continued troubled in her mind until her teacher (Miss Evans) engaged in prayer with the whole of her class. From that time on she gradually attained peace in Jesus.

She has been a Sunday scholar at New Park Street, and afterwards at Tabernacle for thirteen years, ever since she was three years old, the last eight years she has been in Miss Evans' class. This good sister speaks very highly of her and can recommend her to the church. As I have already remarked above, I gave her a card. *Thomas Moor*

I knew this young sister had seen an elder before but who it was I could not discover for the four report books had been taken home by some of the elders. On this evening there were three elders to see enquirers but no single book for them to use. *TM*

She has very little to say, and I think if the messenger sees her several times and instructs her, it will be well. Her brother is a member. Miss Evans recommends her, but she must see Mr Grose before I can propose her, or if proposed he must be messenger. *[The messenger was the elder or deacon who would visit – see page 10.]*

INTERVIEWING ELDERS
Thomas Cook

Thomas Cook was one of the early office bearers who saw many of the enquirers at the start of Spurgeon's ministry. Some of the church officers' names were inscribed on the first stone laid for the building of the new Tabernacle on August 16th, 1859. Spurgeon said at that ceremony: 'I should not wonder, if ever England is destroyed, these relics will find their way into some museum in Australia or America, where they will spell over some of our old-fashioned names, and wonder who ever those good men could be who are inscribed here, as James Low, Samuel Gale, Thomas Olney, Thomas Cook, William Olney, George Winsor, and the like. And I think they will say, "Oh depend upon it, they were some good men or others, and they have put them in stone there." They are living stones indeed, they have served this church well and long. Honour to whom honour is due. I am glad to put their names with mine here; and I hope we shall live together for ever in eternity.'

> **John Robinson**
> 51 Waterloo Street,
> Camberwell

THIS young man had pious parents and was brought up in the Walworth Wesleyan Sunday School. Has mixed in merry company, and though occasionally attending the Music Hall and Tabernacle, had no concern for his soul and often spent his Sabbath in gardening and other things. He states that about six weeks ago the hymn, 'When I survey the wondrous cross &c' fastened itself on his mind. And then he was led to reflect on the great love of Christ, and from that to see what a great sinner he had been. Then he was led to look to Christ, and is resting entirely on him, and he feels and knows that he cannot do anything for himself. He states that he constantly prays for grace that he may live nearer to Christ, and finds that the closer he is to Christ the more happiness he has. He is known to Green and Perkins.

Gave a card. *J W Brown*

I should have preferred that John Robinson had waited rather longer, but I did not feel justified in refusing a seeker to see our pastor so that he might have an opportunity of judging of his statement. There appeared to me in the first instance of getting up a little speech, but I did not wish to think hardly of him, and therefore gave a card. *JWB*

Seems to me a capital sort but messenger may be careful from Mr Brown's hint. *CHS*

> **Sarah Elizabeth Chew**
> 22 Addington Place,
> Camberwell

THIS young friend came with her sister (who also has a card to see our pastor) to testify of God's grace to her. It appears that she has been the subject of serious impressions for the last six years, although at times they wore off, and the pleasures of the world and the ballroom were her delight. In April last she was invited to a party and she with great reluctance went, her conscience telling her it was wrong.

And while there was truly miserable, and resolved in the strength of God from that time to give up these amusements. She then began to pray earnestly to the Lord for forgiveness through the atonement of Christ, and suffering much darkness of mind, until about three weeks since she attended an open-air service while staying at Margate, when a Mr Sulman of Pentonville addressed the congregation and explained the way of salvation, very plainly showing the simplicity of faith in Jesus. And there she was enabled to cast herself wholly upon him and this verse was sung, *which just met her case,* 'Just as I am, without one plea &c'. And she found joy and peace in believing. Our pastor's ministry has also been greatly blessed to her.

A very interesting case. Gave her, *with great pleasure*, a card.

Henry Hanks

> **Sarah Homer**
> 14 Southampton Street,
> Camberwell

THIS sister (who is known to the Miss Chews) has been brought up in the Church of England and all her relatives are much opposed to Dissenters. The work of grace, she states, has been very gradual. When first she heard our pastor at the Music Hall she was fond of worldly amusements, but she soon found she must give up one or the other. And she began to feel the plague of her heart, and sought the Lord for mercy through Christ by earnest prayer, which she believes has been heard and answered, feeling now the burden of sin removed and a simple reliance upon the finished work of Christ. She enjoys solid peace in believing, sometimes enjoys nearness to God in prayer. Also feels an increased hatred to sin, and ascribes the change to sovereign grace alone.

She has heard our pastor for five years, and would have joined before but was not allowed to do so during the grandfather's lifetime. He now being dead, she comes forward to follow the Lord in baptism. Gave her a card.

Henry Hanks

> **John Jennings**
> 15 East Street, Walworth
> Age: 29

THIS young man is quite deaf and dumb, and preaches to the deaf and dumb for some time past. Four years since he heard Mr Vupp who preaches to the deaf and dumb in the Borough Road, and became impressed and very unhappy. He read the Word very much, sat up all night sometimes to read and pray much and wept sorely. Was very unhappy for two or three years, but believes the Spirit brought deliverance to his soul through reading the Word. He now feels much for the souls of others afflicted like himself. Believes salvation to be by grace alone and man's entire helplessness by nature. Believes in final perseverance. Rests alone on the blood and righteousness of Christ for salvation. Believes the ordinance of baptism is set forth plainly in the Word of God and desires to be baptised and obey his Lord's command in the Supper. This is his principal object in wishing to be united to our church.

I find much trouble in understanding him, but believe it is a good case and gave him a card. *George Moore*

EXTRACT FROM CHURCH MEETING BOOK, OCTOBER 16TH 1862

John Jennings preacher to the deaf and dumb came before the church and partly by writing and partly by signs professed his faith in the Lord Jesus Christ and gave a satisfactory account of the work of grace in his soul and the messenger testifying to the excellence of his moral character, it is agreed that he be received as a member in communion with this church after baptism.

John Jennings preacher to the deaf and dumb came before the Church and partley by writing and partley by signs professed his faith in the Lord Jesus Christ and gave a satisfactory account of the work of grace in his soul and the messenger testifying to the excellence of his moral character, it is agreed that he be received as a member in communion with this Church after baptism.

The Tabernacle has a ministry to the deaf today, including a deaf Sunday School. All services are interpreted into British Sign Language and many members have learned BSL to fellowship with deaf friends.

William Kelly
82 Great Guildford Street,
Borough

THIS friend was formerly a scholar in New Park Street Sabbath School (in the late Mr Burgess's class) but when he went out into the world, he went far into sin, and was a great card player until shortly after Mr Spurgeon came to London, when he was induced to attend the ministry, but did not receive any lasting good, until about six years ago. Our pastor preached at the Music Hall from 'Seven Texts'. This completely overpowered him. He was melted to tears of penitence, much distressed on account of his past life. All his old habits he gave up, and the concern of his soul being his first and foremost anxiety. At length in answer to prayer and continued attendance on the ministry, peace and joy was realised, and now is very anxious to follow Christ in baptism. He is well known to our Brother Tucker. I cheerfully gave him a card.

Henry Hanks

'Confession of Sin – A Sermon With Seven Texts' (113) preached Sunday January 18th 1857 at the Music Hall, Royal Surrey Gardens. 'I have sinned.' *(Exodus 9.27)*

Mary Ann Edwards
2 Craven Cottage,
Loughborough Road,
Brixton

THIS young person refers with much feeling to the dying prayers of her godly mother which she says that, although she was then very young, she has never been permitted to forget, although she strove for years to do so, everything of a religious character being then particularly obnoxious to her. She hated the instruction of her pious father. About four years since came, in the providence of God, to London to reside, and at that time entered the New Park Street Sunday School. But her heart remained hard and impenitent until she heard our pastor preach the sermon on the 'Three Lepers'. The Word came with power to her heart, and brought her into deep distress lest God should at once call her to judgement for her sin. She remained in a state of mind bordering on despair for some months, until she heard Mr Spurgeon preach at Clapham from, 'And Jesus stood and cried, If any man thirst &c'. This was a peculiarly blessed season to her. Light broke in upon her soul and she was enabled to put her trust in the atoning blood of Christ. Her mourning was turned into rejoicing.

Is still looking alone to Jesus. Finds the preached Word much blessed to her soul and also the instruction she receives in Mrs Bartlett's class. I had much conversation with her, was greatly pleased with the evidence she gave of a change of heart and with her doctrinal knowledge. Gave a card. *William Perkins*

John Frost
29 Alford St, Grange Road

AN earnest follower of Jesus Christ. Was a member of the Wesleyan body at Milbourne Port, Somerset. On his coming to London attended the Southwark Chapel. All went on well for a time until about fifteen months since, when the class leader asked him if he had read Spurgeon's sermon. He replied, 'Which one?' The leader said, 'Oh, the one he preached last Sunday morning, I never heard such damnable doctrine in my life. Surely Spurgeon will damn all the souls to hell that hear him.' The leader lent him this 'shocking' sermon to read. (Bless the Lord for it.) He read it and returned it to the leader.

From this time his eyes were opened. He saw at once our dear pastor's preaching was in strict accordance with the Word of Truth, and at once did not shun to declare the same. This aroused the leader, who said, 'If you believe such damnable doctrine, you had better to go to him at once.' He has regularly attended the preaching of the Word ever since. (An interesting case.) *W B Hackett*

Mary Ann Jones
31 Kirby St, Hatton Garden

IN the summer of 1861 she came out of curiosity to hear Mr Spurgeon on a weeknight service, merely that she might be able to say that she had heard him. The text was 'The queen of the south shall rise up in judgement &c'. 'Oh,' she said, 'when I came out of the Tabernacle, I wished I had never gone. I was afraid, I trembled and determined I would never go again, especially as I had been accustomed to work at my employment on Sundays. But I felt miserable at staying away, so I gave up the Sunday work and came again. It was still the same for months. I was miserable if I came, and miserable when I stayed away. Until at last I found Christ, and with him peace and comfort. But I did not find him until I gave up seeking peace in everything else, and I think I tried almost everything first.'

I saw her last autumn and sent her to Mrs Moor's class for more instruction. This night she comes again, and with great pleasure I gave her a card.

Thomas Moor

Eliza Gardner
88 St George's Road

WAS awakened four years ago under the preaching of Mr Spurgeon, but her mode of living (keeping a beer shop) was a great hindrance to her. Three years ago this was given up and although she continued to attend the ministry of the Word, she did not obtain joy and peace in believing until November last when Mr Spurgeon preached on the subject 'Food for the hungry'. She has had many trials in providence. Some troubles have surrounded her path but Christ is her light and joy in all.

> **'Bread for the Hungry'**
> (418) preached Sunday November 10th 1861 at the Metropolitan Tabernacle. 'And he humbled thee, and suffered thee to hunger…that he might make thee know that man doth not live by bread only, but by every word that proceedeth out of the mouth of the Lord.'
> *(Deuteronomy 8.3)*

Thomas Moor

Keeps a lady's wardrobe shop – Mr Pearce the tailor to be seen.

Her husband has a cab on our rank and comes here. Wants to be looked after. Cab 10797.

A note added by William Olney. One of the converts he saw that evening was Alice Tatnell, on opposite page, along with three other members of her family.

'On this evening I felt greater pleasure in the cases that came before me than I almost ever remember before. All the cases are clear and good. Every one of them has some particular interest in it. And the fact of four of one family coming at one time is I believe a fact almost unparalleled in our church history. God is evidently working mightily in our midst as a church. To his name be all the glory.'

Abraham Coutis
33 Downham Road, Islington
[Late a student at
the Borough Road]

THIS young man was first impressed at Devonport while on a visit last July, by one of his friends speaking to him of the love of Christ. He went to see Mr Stock (of that town) to converse with him on spiritual things. On his return to London, one of his fellow students invited him to attend Brother Hanks' class. He came to please others and returned as he came, although he has never lost the impression made on his mind.

In a few days the Lord laid his afflicting hand upon him and he was confined to his bed for three weeks. During this time, he was much in prayer and meditation. He states during this affliction, he was convicted of sin and sought Jesus earnestly. After hearing our pastor on the first Sabbath evening, when he reached home, he asked his good brother to spend a short time with him in prayer. Believing alone in Christ, he felt the load of guilt fall off, and he found pardon.

Gave a card.

William Hackett

Alice Tatnell

WAS brought to know and love the Lord by a sermon of our pastor's in which he especially addressed the unconverted children of Christian persons, telling them how great their condemnation if they neglected the salvation of their souls. She went home at once and sought forgiveness in prayer, and believes she found peace and salvation through the blood and merits of Jesus. Is looking only to him for salvation. Old things with her have passed away, and all things have become new. She has a full and clear understanding of the doctrines of grace, and is able to give a very clear and satisfactory account of the work of grace in her heart. Hers is a very decided and interesting case of conversion to God. Gave a card with very great pleasure.

William Olney

Joseph Summersum
7 Providence Row,
Finsbury Square

CANNOT date his conversion but believes it attributable humanly speaking to his elder brother, aged 33, who was a very pious and at the same time intellectual man, master of six languages – among which were Hebrew and Greek. This elder brother made it his chief duty to instruct him and his sister in the things pertaining to eternity, and he tells me that, like Doddridge, he learnt the parables and miracles of Christ from the Dutch tiles of his parents' fireplace. His brother, however, being called away to some work at Lanark, he fell away and gradually settled into infidelity – reading the work of Voltaire, Payne &c. But the Lord graciously restored him to a full sense of his pardoning love. Our pastor's ministry has been very much blessed to him. He was introduced to me by our Brother Line – his testimony was *very voluminous* – so much so that I found it difficult to compress it, and he kept me in such close conversation that I could not put down all my notes. But I was well satisfied with him and gave a card. *Frederick Grose*

Henry Akehurst
3 New Park Road,
Brixton Hill

THIS friend is indeed a monument of sovereign grace and another seal to the ministry of our beloved pastor, but let his own words testify. He was in early life brought up in the Church of England, and at the age of fourteen he was about to be confirmed. And in the preparatory services he was told that up to that time his godfather and godmother were answerable for those sins that he had committed, but from that time he would himself be answerable for his sins in future. And he says, he was horror struck and refused to be confirmed, for in looking at the ten commandments, he felt he had broken them all, and that hell must be his position, and that he could not answer for one sin in a thousand. He went on very unhappy, feeling himself to be a sinner but did not know the remedy.

A long time after this he heard Mr James Spurgeon at Brixton, and was then told our pastor was going to preach in the Music Hall. He went on the first night but could not get in. He

'Confession and Absolution'
(216) preached Sunday October 3rd 1858 at the Music Hall, Royal Surrey Gardens. 'And the publican, standing afar off, would not lift up so much as his eyes unto heaven, but smote upon his breast, saying, God be merciful to me a sinner.'
(Luke 18.13)

went again when the subject was the prayer of the publican, 'God be merciful to me a sinner.' When our pastor at the close of the sermon wished all those who could join with him in this prayer should after him say audibly 'Amen', he was one, who from his broken heart said 'Amen'. He was overpowered with grief and tears. He continued to attend every service but in great distress of mind – unbelief was so strong, and that he was too great a sinner to be saved. And that he must feel or do something that God would accept, or that Christ must work some special miracle for him before he could find peace or salvation.

He sometime afterwards heard our pastor preach at Park Crescent Chapel from these words, 'Him that is athirst let him come unto me and drink.' This was the time of love to his soul. Our pastor concluded by supposing a case. A command being sent from the Queen to a very poor man to come directly to the palace, 'to come just as you are, and to stay away at your peril'. The man instead of obeying the command, is going about to get better clothes and making himself fit to go, and he reads the command again, 'Come as you are.' Now the Spirit of God applied this to his soul and he was enabled to fly to Christ with these words, 'Just as I am, without one plea, but that thy blood was shed for me &c.' He saw then that he had been trying to prepare himself instead of coming vile and unworthy as he was. 'Come just as you are.' He was enabled to do so, and now he is trusting and rejoicing in the finished work of Christ for him.

This was the seventh and last case I had this evening, but I felt that I could have sat all night to have heard the brother's expression of his love to Jesus for his amazing grace manifested to one so unworthy. Glory be to God. Gave him a card.

Henry Hanks

Charles Dalton Bloodworth
39 Durham Street, Kennington Lane

HAD heard of the accident at Surrey Gardens Music Hall and was induced out of curiosity to attend. And by hearing our pastor preach, it led him to think and to search the Scriptures, and to enquire in them about the Lord Jesus and about his own state. 'And from the first time I came, I could never give up attending the house of God.' But owing to his being at that time in a business which was a great hindrance to his growth in grace, he found that God and mammon would not do together. So he got out of it, and resolved in the strength of the Lord to seek his kingdom first, and give himself entirely into the hands of the Holy Spirit, which he found was leading him a different way to that in which he had ever been before. And now he rests only on Jesus and desires only to live to him.

The work has been gradual. He had no sudden impressions but he is certain that what he feels and enjoys is only the work of God. And the seventh and eighth chapters of *Romans* he can read over and over again, and the truth therein revealed corresponds greatly with his own experience, and enjoys a peace which flows from a sense of blood-bought pardon. Was thoroughly satisfied with his testimony and gave a card. *John Ward*

Jane Hill
53 Chester Street,
Kennington Lane

THIS person has always been in the habit of attending the service of the Church of England, and most frequently Mr Hussay of Brixton. She says she was taken ill and lost her reason for fifteen months, but the goodness of God was here manifest when reason returned, came also a sense of sin. Was very anxious about her soul. Came to hear our pastor. Many sermons have been blessed to her, but 'one appeal' of our pastor's proved a blessing to her and enabled her to put her trust in Jesus. She is now relying upon the righteousness of Christ for her acceptance with God. Wishes to be baptised to shew her love to Jesus. Gave a card. *Mr Roe*

Recommended to the class. She is a good girl. What a marvel that madness should be the servant of grace.

At wholesale house Vyse and Son, Wood Street *[makers of straw hats at Cheapside]* all day long and only home in the evening.

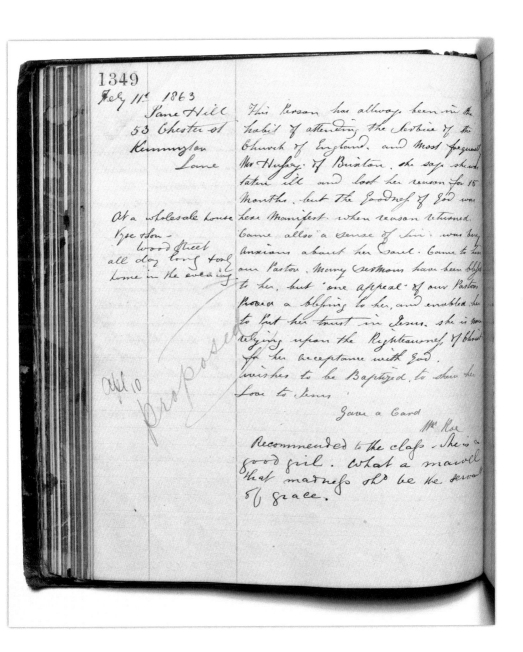

1349

Feby 11th 1863

Jane Hill
53 Chester st
Kennington
Lane

At a wholesale House
Vyse + Son —
Wood street
all day long + at
home in the evening

Apl 10 Proposed

This Person has allways been in the habit of attending the Service of the Church of England. and most frequently Mr Hussey. of Buxton. she says she was taken ill and lost her reason for 15 Months. but the Goodness of God was here Manifest. when reason returned. Came allso a sense of Sin. was very anxious about her Soul. Came to hear our Pastor. Many Sermons have been blessed to her, but "one appeal" of our Pastor proved a blessing to her, and enabled her to put her trust in Jesus. she is now relying upon the Righteousness of Christ for her acceptance with God. wishes to be Baptized, to shew her Love to Jesus

Gave a Card

Mr Roe

Recommended to the class. She is a good girl. What a marvel that madness shd be the servant of grace.

A reduced size photograph of the testimony to the left.
(The size of the original books is 21cm wide by 25cm tall.)

1365   March 24 - 1863

Edward Overett
50 Beech St   Is in the employment
     Barbican   of our Bro Lawrence —
                          Had lived a very sinful life
gone into the greatest depths of Sin & wholly
neglected the means of grace — His ex-
=cesses had made his home very unhappy
on one occasion on a Sabbath day ^in last August
having quarreled with his wife he left home
& wandering about — remembered that his
employer Mr Lawrence had often wished him
to go & hear our Pastor at that moment the name
of Mr Spurgeon in large letters on a placard arrested
his attention & he at once determined to go and
hear him — did so — felt interested — came again
until in a few weeks under the sermon from
"Thy Brother's Blood &c." the Lord was pleased to show
him his sin & his need of a Saviour & also to show
him his total inability to do anything toward his
own salvation — continued for two or three
months in great soul trouble — his relish for
& enjoyment of the preached word however on each
occasion continued to increase & gradually
faith was given him to look alone to Jesus
& he obtained peace — once he was afraid
of God now he loves to draw near to him —
Prayers earnestly for Sanctification of heart &
conformity to the mind & will of Christ
— with much pleasure gave a card
                              Wm Perkins

(margin note) lived three years with Lawrence & only goes to his home on a Sunday for an hour or two. —

A reduced size photograph of the testimony to the right. Report here written by
William Perkins, with a note in the margin added in Spurgeon's handwriting.
(The size of the original books is 21 cm wide by 25 cm tall.)

The elders' room at the Metropolitan Tabernacle, 1861

Edward Overett
50 Bewick Street, Barbican

IS in the employment of our Brother Lawrence. Had lived a very sinful life, gone into the greatest depths of sin, and wholly neglected the means of grace. His excesses had made his home very unhappy. On one occasion on a Sabbath in last August, having quarrelled with his wife, he left home and wandering about remembered that his employer Mr Lawrence had often wished him to go and hear our pastor. At that moment the name of Mr Spurgeon in large letters on a placard arrested his attention, and he at once determined to go and hear him. Did so, felt instructed, came again, until in a few weeks under the sermon from 'Thy brother's blood &c', the Lord was pleased to show him his sin and his need of a Saviour, and also to show him his total inability to do anything toward his own salvation. Continued for two or three months in great soul trouble. His relish for and enjoyment of the preached Word, however, on each occasion continued to increase, and gradually faith was given him to look alone to Jesus, and he obtained peace. Once he was afraid of God, now he loves to draw near to him. Prays earnestly for sanctification of heart, and conformity to the mind and will of Christ.

> **'Am I Clear of his Blood?'**
> (461) preached Sunday July 20th 1862 at the Metropolitan Tabernacle. 'The voice of thy brother's blood crieth unto me from the ground.'
> *(Genesis 4.10)*

With much pleasure gave a card.

William Perkins

Lived three years with Lawrence, and only goes to his home on a Sunday for an hour or two.

> **William Wiggins**
> 12 Perry Street, Brompton
> (youth)

WANTS to join the membership but does not attend Tab. He is very chatty. Has very little knowledge, but apparently a great deal of self-satisfaction. He cannot attend Mr Hanks' class, and thinks Mr Roye's too dry for him. He seems to have only half an ear but *seven tongues.*

Thomas Moor

This 'youth' applied for admission to the College. Recommended him to the evening classes; he attended for a short time. I think the above a very accurate description. *CB*

> **Harriet Harman**
> 2 Park Cottage, Park Street, Kennington Cross

ABOUT eleven months ago lost her mother very suddenly by death. This sudden bereavement was greatly blessed to the awakening of her conscience. She felt she was a lost sinner and went to Christ, aspiring for forgiveness. She soon found peace through his blood. She came to hear our pastor. Here she found just what she wanted – the Bread of Life that alone the soul can feed on. A few weeks ago she was much encouraged by an invitation from Mr Spurgeon, 'Come just as you are &c'. Our pastor described her case exactly, and she stated she can say she is resting wholly on the finished work of Christ.

She has a very heavy trial. Her husband *(one of the best)* is a cabman and drives on the Sabbath. So anxious is he to hear the Gospel, he very often leaves his cab on the stand in charge that he may come in and hear the sermon. Gave a card.

W B Hackett

Cab drivers were not allowed to leave their cab unattended when parked at a stand – it had to be left 'in charge', with someone to look after it. The Earl of Shaftesbury set up a Cabman's Shelter Fund to provide cabbies with shelters and refreshments. (Courtesy: LSE Library)

> **Jemima Hutchins**
> 22 Webbs County Terrace,
> New Kent Road

USED to live an utterly careless and irreligious life, though not humanly-speaking immoral. Was led by curiosity to come to the Tabernacle to the opening services. Her parents both ungodly, and also she at this time was living with ungodly people. Soon after this however she lived with a family who had seats at the Tabernacle but are not members, with whom she enjoyed religious privileges in the family, which were a great help to her.

On the 17th of May last, the Word came with power to her soul. She does not remember the text (and not being able to read, the printed sermon was of little use to her) but the pastor was speaking about sinners coming to Christ, particularly something about setting up a white and a red flag, and he said, 'Which will you pull down?'

She believes that God has answered her prayers and saved her soul. *Christ alone* is her hope of salvation. She felt that her sins were great, but all settled for and *done* away in the person and by the work of Jesus. She can no longer mix in the world, but only with the people of God can she find *any* pleasure. She attends Mrs Bartlett's class and finds great profit therefrom. Believes baptism the duty of a believer.

I was much pleased with this sister and especially at the solicitude she evinced for the salvation of her mother. Her father is dead. Before he died, strange to say, she tried to point him to a Saviour, whom she says *that at the time* she did not know for herself. I gave a card. *Frederick Grose*

> **Watson Prime**
> 2 New Cut, Lambeth

HAD lived an outwardly moral life but had for several years neglected the means of grace. Had constantly kept open his shop on the Sabbath, as did many others in his neighbourhood. At length they agreed amongst themselves to close their shops on the Sabbath. On the first Sabbath went to hear our pastor (this is three years since) at Exeter Hall. In that place the Lord awakened him under the sermon from 'The wicked shall be turned into hell &c'. The burden of sin was heavy upon him for some days. On the following Thursday evening heard Mr S at New Park Street. He was preaching an encouraging sermon to young believers. Under it he found peace. Has few doubts but has many sweet seasons of communion with Christ, these are indeed his happiest moments. Is looking wholly to Christ for grace, strength and perseverance. Desires to be baptised in obedience to the Saviour.

> **'Tender Words of Terrible Apprehension!'**
> (344) preached Sunday November 4th 1860 at Exeter Hall, Strand. 'The wicked shall be turned into hell, and all the nations that forget God.'
> *(Psalm 9.17)*

Was much pleased with his testimony and gave him a card.

William Perkins

This friend would have come forward earlier but has been waiting hoping to induce his wife to come with him, believing her to be truly converted to God. This he has been unable to do at present but hopes to bring her soon.

> **Henry Oxford**
> 31 Pair Street, Horselydown
> Age: 16

ABOUT last April twelvemonth went to a friend's house, who used to attend our pastor's ministry. His object in going was, primarily, to show off a new suit of clothes he had got on. This friend, who was a friend *indeed*, brought him to the Tabernacle, and he felt some relish for the service, but the breaking of the heart was reserved for our Brother Richard Weaver. He went a Sunday or two afterwards to the Surrey Theatre and came away crying out like the Philippian Gaoler, 'What shall I do &c.' This did not last long, for in the beginning of May the truth dawned upon his soul gradually that faith in the work of Christ was the great, the only thing needful; that simply to believe and to trust in what Christ had done was salvation.

Ever since he has found Christ precious to him. He has not the least doubt of his conversion. He enjoys prayer and the reading of the Word and the service of God, whereas once he lived far away, reading novels on the Lord's Day and seeking all sorts of worldly pleasures. 'Old things have passed away, all things become new.' The sermon on 'Lead us not into temptation' was very useful to him.

> **'Lead Us Not Into Temptation'** (509) preached Sunday May 17th 1863 at the Metropolitan Tabernacle. 'Lead us not into temptation, but deliver us from evil.' *(Matthew 6.13)*

I questioned this young man very closely upon many of the doctrines and found him for the most part to have now clear views of truth, and I believe him to be sincere. With pleasure, I gave a card.

Frederick Grose

> **Elizabeth Barnett**
> 16 Emma Street, Annes Place, Hackney Road

THIS sister's experience is a good commentary upon the text, 'I am sought of them that asked not for me, *I am found of them that sought me not.*' Our sister was, until lately, the only one of her family not converted, her father, mother and brothers being members of Mr Russell's church, where she also used to attend. She used to stifle what convictions she used to feel, for at some Tuesday night meetings that were held there she often felt convictions of sin. Our good sister Sarah Nay, who worked with her, was constantly importuning her to come and hear our pastor, but she would not. At length as they were returning one day from the Exhibition our good sister Nay caught her by guile. It was on a cloudy night and, to use her own words, 'she dragged her in', for she most resolutely persisted in it for some time that she would *not* come in.

One Sunday evening the sermon upon the lepers, 'Where are the nine?' pricked her to the heart. She went home praying that she might not be one of the nine, for having put off so many opportunities of glorifying God she thought she must be. When she went home, she fell on her knees before God and before she rose from them the Lord gave her a sweet manifestation of peace and joy. She was, however, afraid this was merely natural feeling. She therefore prayed for a further manifestation

> **'Where Are the Nine? Where?'**
> (2960) preached in the year 1863 at the Metropolitan Tabernacle. 'And Jesus answering said, Were there not ten cleansed? but where are the nine?' *(Luke 17.17)*

when the texts – 'I love them that love me and they that seek me early shall find me' and 'I will never leave thee nor forsake thee' – were powerfully applied to her soul.

A good case, well taught in Scripture and doctrine. With great pleasure, I gave a card.

Frederick Grose

> **Mercy Hanks**
> 9 Lorrimore Terrace, and 5 & 6 Walworth Road

IS the daughter of our dear Brother Hanks, and having been privileged with pious parents and sitting under a searching and faithful ministry, has often been the subject of convictions, but these soon wore off and were, time after time, forgotten.

Under the sermon 'And yet there is room', a more abiding work was commenced. The guilt of so long neglecting truly to seek the mercy and forgiveness of God through Jesus Christ was shown her, and also the wondrous kindness and longsuffering of God that even for her 'yet there was room'. The same evening, her father's prayer was much blessed to her. Still for a month or more she continued in much darkness, when the Lord was pleased to give her light and joy in believing on him.

The fulness of the assurance of her acceptance in Christ was not given her until she heard our pastor from 'How answered the ambassadors &c'. Has now no other trust than the blood and righteousness of the Redeemer. Knows she loves the Saviour and desires to walk in his footsteps. Her testimony being simple and clear, I gave a card with great pleasure. *William Perkins*

> **James Stanley**
> 5 Amelia Street,
> Walworth Road

THIS aged brother has long worshipped with us. He was a seat holder in Mr Smith's* time at New Park Street, and has heard our pastor constantly. He evidently has long had a love for the ways of Zion, but there always seemed such hindrances and obstacles in the way that he could not overcome. He experiences strong opposition in his family, so much so that he has to shut himself up in a shed in the yard for prayer and reading the Word. He believes he experienced a divine change from the time when our pastor addressed the congregation to ask the question, 'Am I a child of God?' He went home again to ask the Lord for the witness of his Spirit, and he believes that now he has passed from death unto life.

> The story of Jack the Huckster, 'a poor, wicked fellow', is told in 'Christ's Prayer for His People' (47) preached Sunday October 21st 1855. 'I'm a poor sinner and nothing at all, but Jesus Christ is my all-in-all.'

He says Jack the Huckster's language will suit him – 'I'm a poor sinner and nothing at all &c.' I am fully assured that this is the Spirit's work in him and therefore gave a card. *Henry Hanks*

> **Mr George Thomas**
> at Hitchcocks and Co,
> St Paul's

THIS young man dates his conversion on November 27th 1861 during the prayer meeting after business *[at his work place]*. He had often been invited to unite at the meeting. That evening he accepted the invitation and the Lord met him and from that hour has found

---

* The Rev James Smith was pastor at New Park Street from 1841 to 1850, before moving to Cheltenham to take up a pastorate there. He is the author of the *Daily Remembrancer* still in print today.

FIELD LANE RAGGED SCHOOL,
WEST ST HOLBORN HILL.

Field Lane Ragged School referred to below was founded by the London City Mission in 1841. Lord Shaftesbury supported it lifelong, being president of the Ragged School Union for 39 years. Spurgeon gave much help to the Ragged Schools, many Tabernacle members founding and labouring in such Schools. The secretary of the Ragged School Union at the time said that there was scarcely a School in London which did not have workers from the Tabernacle. One of the elders mentioned in these reports, John Dunn, founded the mission room and Ragged School in Richmond Street, Walworth, which later became East Street Baptist Church. (Courtesy: London Metropolitan Archives, City of London)

peace. Up to this time went like others to church. Now he found the food he took before would not satisfy his hunger. At last came to the Tabernacle. Here he felt at home. It was the precious pearl he had been seeking, and he found it in the Christ-like sermons of our pastor. He has regularly attended the Tabernacle since on the morning of the Lord's Day. In the afternoon he sows the Word by giving away tracts, and in the evening engaged at Field Lane Ragged School. He is a young man full of love for Jesus and anxious to bring others to know and love his Master.

William Hackett

Charles Jeffrey
7 Penton Place, Walworth

THIS poor man about four months since came wishing to join the church with his wife, but they both seemed so confused in their views as to the way of salvation that I wished them both to wait, urging upon them to seek by prayer for the Holy Spirit's teaching. They now both come and have evidently grown in grace and their simple testimony of faith in Jesus is very satisfactory. This brother thanks me for wishing him to wait and states that now he feels a new creature. The public house he has forsaken and abhors, as well as pleasure-taking on Sundays, the house of God and his service being his delight. He knows very little of the doctrines, but he believes God has begun a good work in his soul and will perfect it. He hates sin, and prayer is his constant habit. I was much pleased with his apparent sincerity and gave him a card.

Henry Hanks

Hannah Jeffrey
7 Penton Place, Walworth

THIS friend came to see me about four months ago at which time, although evidently anxious about her soul yet had such confused views of the way of salvation that I wished her to wait, encouraging her to seek the Lord by earnest prayer and reading the Word.

It appeared about two years since she received serious impressions and conviction of sin from hearing our pastor. These were not lasting as she used to go with her husband on Sundays on the water occasionally. But the last time she went she was most miserable and said that if they got home safe, she would never go again. And now the house of God and his people are her choice.

She has also derived much comfort and instruction from services held at the Cabmen's Club. The singing of the hymn, 'There is a fountain filled with blood &c' was greatly blessed to her. Also it appears when she began to seek the Lord, she could not read but such has been her anxiety to read and understand the Scriptures *that she has taught herself to read,* so that the Word and promises of God are her daily comfort. I am quite satisfied she is trusting alone upon Christ. Gave her a card. *Henry Hanks*

John William Taylor
21 Havil Terrace,
Willow Walk, Bermondsey

THIS youth, 19 years of age, is engaged in the Counting House at 'Christies'. It appears about twelve months ago he received serious impressions, and was obliged to give up his water excursions on the Sabbath and attend regularly the Tabernacle. The Word has evidently been much blessed to him. He is very thoughtful and somewhat reserved, but his answers are very clear and satisfactory. He states prayer and reading the Word are his delight, which is proved by having, with another youth employed with him, established a prayer meeting in the warehouse before commencing business in the morning, several attending with them. He has just lost a sister who used to attend the Tabernacle and died very happy. She spoke very affectionately to him and hoped to meet him in Heaven. This, with the preaching of the Word by our pastor, has brought him to decide for God and confess his name.

A very satisfactory case. Gave him a card.

Henry Hanks

Frederick G S Norris
183 Albany Road, Camberwell
Ship owner's clerk
Messrs Shallen, Dale & Co.,
38 Carsenhill

THIS brother was first led to attend our pastor's ministry at the Surrey Music Hall by his wife's sister, much against his own will. The impressions made on his mind were favourable. He has attended here nearly as long as the Tabernacle has been opened, and this has been his second birthplace. Through the ministry of our pastor he has been convicted of sin, and has found peace in Jesus but cannot mention any particular sermon. He seems to be only relying upon the blood and righteousness of Jesus. He believes his wife to be

Elephant & Castle looking south, 1900
(Courtesy: London Metropolitan Archives, City of London)

a true Christian. She has been greatly blessed to him as an instructor and leader, and yet he has come forward first.

Desires to be baptised. Gave him a card. *W B Collins*

Owes much to the Bible which he reads with care, and also to the example of Miss Goodwin, one of our members. What an honour to holiness to become this useful. Friend Perkins to see the good wife and talk with her a little. Mr N is not at home till the evening. *CHS*

Henrietta Hope
16 George Street,
Trafalgar Street,
Walworth

THIS good sister was brought up in the Church of England, and about fifteen years ago applied to the parish priest to be confirmed. No certificate of her sprinkling could be found, and was told she must be sprinkled afresh before she could be confirmed. Although on this occasion she was told she was regenerated, no peace of soul could she obtain. Being now more unhappy than before, she went to various churches to hear the Word but no comfort could she obtain. Some long time since, a neighbour said to her, 'If you want to hear a good sermon and the Gospel of Jesus Christ come with me to hear Mr Dunn at the Mission Room.' This was very humbling to her but still she went. And to the joy of her soul here she found the pearl of great price. The text was 'Jesus Christ, the same yesterday, today and forever'. She went home, and soon found all her good works were but filthy rags. No one can tell the deep sorrow she felt on account of sin. She knows it is all done for her by her precious Saviour. I was much pleased with her and gave her a card.

W B Hackett

Edward W Smith
141 King's Road,
Chelsea

THIS youth is the brother of James Smith, now a member of this church. His former habits were similar to his brother's. A Pedestrian* or a 'Runner'. It seems last November he was persuaded by his brother (who had earnestly prayed for him since his own conversion) to attend the Tabernacle and the catechumen class. Our young brethren Yost and Morgan noticed him, took him aside in one of the rooms in the Tabernacle, and prayed for him and exhorted him to faith and repentance. This seems to have been the means of his *at once* forsaking all his former habits and associates, and seeking the Lord by prayer, pleading the blood of Jesus for forgiveness – which he feels he has experienced. He regularly attends the class, prayer is his delight, even in his work he must pray, and has found peace in believing. I think this is another proof of the sovereignty and freeness of God's grace. Gave him a card.

Henry Hanks

A shop kept by Mr Lawrence, a ham and beef shop, works long and late. Quite a boy to look at but is 19 years of age. *CHS*

---

* Pedestrianism was competitive walking funded by gambling.

T Fowler
8 Johns Terrace,
Southampton St, Camberwell
Cartloads at Mr Westrope Stables,
36 Southampton Street
Looks after horse and cart

THIS brother was first led to attend a cottage meeting held in Mrs Coult's house through the earnest request of this good sister, and while reading the first verse, chapter 8 of *Romans*, the Word went home with power to his heart, and he shortly afterwards found peace through the same Word, which killed and made alive.

His previous life had been very sinful.

Attends Mr Hanks' class, desires to be baptised. Gave him a card. *W B Collins*

One of an unconverted family, a token of distinguishing grace. He is changed as a workman and is an eye-server no more. He has had answers to prayer, lost a former place through refusing to work on Sundays but prayer found him another place. *CHS*

Caroline Elizabeth Rooks
8 Isabella Row,
Mansion House Street,
Kennington Road

THIS young woman has long been waiting to be received into the church, and whose case has caused myself and our sister, Mrs Bartlett *[see panel to right],* much anxiety, feeling assured of her sincerity and yet in conversation, through ignorance would say and unsay what she knew of the way of salvation and her ground of acceptance with God. We have therefore wished her to wait, still encouraging her and teaching her the truth as it is in Jesus.

Some few months ago, she fell down the gallery stairs and broke her arm, which affliction has been greatly sanctified. And I have been much pleased with my last interview, and believe her to be a child of God and very anxious to follow the Lord in obedience to his command. Gave her a card. *Henry Hanks*

Seems a most faithful and regular hearer and I think a most sincere believer. *CHS*

William Baverstock
8 Brook Street,
Kennington Road

CAME first to hear our pastor on the Sunday evening after the death of Prince Albert. Before that was living quite a careless, irreligious life, although kept from very immoral outward sins. He always thought religion a dull, mopish thing, but has had great reason to alter his opinion. Has never felt so happy since he came to hear the Gospel, and feels that a thorough change has been

'A Cure for Care'
(428) preached Sunday January 12th 1862 at the Metropolitan Tabernacle. 'Casting all your care upon him; for he careth for you.'
(1 Peter 5.7)

wrought in him. The sermon upon 'Casting all your care upon him' was blessed to him. He had long wished to join, but thought that a

Mrs Lavinia Bartlett's Bible class grew over the years from just a handful to over 700 older girls and working young women on her class roll, many of whom were servants with very little education. A church report for Mrs Bartlett's class commented – 'The question has often been asked by Sabbath School teachers with painful anxiety, How shall we retain our senior scholars? How shall we prevent their going away from religious influences just when they most need them? They can be laid hold of by earnest and devoted teachers at that critical period.' Many young women from her class applied for baptism and membership.

great deal of preparation was necessary, and that he must come up to a certain standard of perfection before he could join the church. He thought he was *not good enough* nor his faith *strong enough*. His whole trust is in Christ and what he has done for guilty sinners.

I was satisfied with this brother's testimony. He has a moderate knowledge of doctrine. Gave a card.

Frederick Grose

Emily J Bingley
79 New Street, Princes Road,
Kennington Cross
Age: 17

STATES that sometime since, our pastor gave an address to the Sabbath School and spoke of the importance of early giving the heart to the Lord. On leaving the class, her teacher said 'Emily, when will you give your heart to the Lord?' This aroused her to see her lost and ruined state. Soon after heard our pastor preach from the text 'Come up hither'. This sermon set her soul at liberty, and she heard her Saviour say to her, 'I have loved thee with an everlasting love.'

'The Voice From Heaven'
(488) preached Sunday November 23rd 1862 at the Metropolitan Tabernacle. 'And they heard a great voice from heaven saying unto them, Come up hither.' *(Revelation 11.12)*

Her statement is very simple but clear, and trusting alone on the righteousness of Christ. I felt I must give her a card to see our pastor.

W B Hackett

Her ungodly parents are much opposed to her coming to the Tabernacle.

Amelia Fult
29 Little Union Street,
Borough Road

WAS induced to attend the Tabernacle by two gentlemen from the Tabernacle. She did not know their names. They lent herself and her husband their cards – was seriously impressed under the ministry and saw herself to be a sinner in the sight of God. A sermon on

Christ's sufferings made a deep impression on her and she cried to God to save her. And she believes he has heard her cry, and she has found peace by believing in him, trusts in his blood alone for salvation.

This poor woman has an irreligious husband, and he occasionally breaks out through drink, and has great struggles to maintain her family, but her trust is in God. I made many enquiries of her about her affairs to endeavour to sift her, but did not detect anything that would lead me to doubt her sincerity, but deferred giving her a card till I had heard the testimony of the friends who visited.

John Ward

Having had an excellent testimony from the brethren who had been visiting her, gave her a card. *John Ward*

NB – This sister has called on me to tell me while she was out at work, her children destroyed Mr Blackshaw's note, and would feel obliged for another invitation to meet Mr S (a good case).

James Ballands
31 Goldsmith Row,
Hackney Road

THIS brother has been brought to know the Lord through his wife, who is a member with us. Her godly life and conversation has had great weight. It has been a gradual change with him. Our pastor has also been a means of great blessing to him, and he seems to owe his final declaring to a few words spoken after the communion service about eight months since. He was sitting in the gallery, and our pastor said, 'Zaccheus, come down,' which seemed to impress his mind that he ought to come down and sit with his wife, who was then in the area at the communion.

He is alone trusting to Christ, now he believes his soul is saved, and that if he were now to die it would be to be present with the Lord.

Desires to be baptised. Gave him a card.

W B Collins

> **Thomas Apps**
> 23 Alfred Street, Mile End
> Pipemaker, worked nearly a
> twelvemonth for Mr Bason.
> Not home till 9.

HAS been under convictions of sin from infancy, though until lately he could neither read nor write, but he strove against the work of the Spirit. And thus he went on, some-time sinning, and sometime repenting, but on the whole striving against conviction. But lately his greatest grief has been that he had sinned away the grace God has given him. But it pleased God about three years since to lay him on a bed of affliction, and that was the means God used to humble him and convince him of sin. And still he endeavoured to resist, till coming a twelvemonth ago to hear our pastor, the fetters were broken under the sermon when Mr S was describing the breaking of a flint stone, rather than an Indian rubber

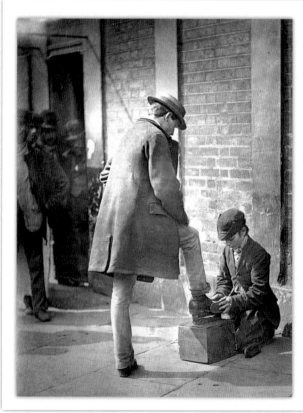

'His mother has to nurse an invalid husband, and must also provide for a large family. Under these circumstances, it was not always easy for her to spare the services of her son. But when he became an independent bootblack, he could go out at his own hours, and thus was of greater use to his mother in her trouble; and it was a great help to the family to know that whenever the boy had a few moments to spare, he might run out and hope to gain some pence by cleaning gentlemen's boots.' From the book *Street Life in London* by John Thomson, published in 1876-7. (Courtesy: LSE Library)

ball. He felt it applied to his case, and from that time he has felt a peace never enjoyed by him before. He now rests on nothing but the Lord Jesus himself. He now sees his election. He now feels he could die for the Lord Jesus Christ. He is much tormented among his work fellows, but he prays the Lord to keep him in temptation. The ministry of our pastor exactly meets his case, and he has learned to read so that the Word is like music to his soul.

Gave him a card.

John Ward

Brown to see this wonder of grace on Sunday between services. *CHS*

> **Ada Stickland**
> At Madame Lusignand's
> 15 Rockingham Row,
> New Kent Road
> Age: 16

IN Mrs Shepherd's class in the Sabbath School, and strongly recommended by her. Was first convinced of sin at a prayer meeting about fifteen months ago from an earnest address of Mr Spurgeon appealing to sinners. Her conviction of sin lasted very long, and she did not find Christ till our pastor preached on the 'Shepherd and his lambs'. She then felt a personal interest in the Saviour, and it was to her soul a time of joy and peace. She then realised fully that she might come, and then surrendered her heart fully to Jesus. Since then her joy and peace has been full, and finds all the

> **'The Lambs and their Shepherd'**
> (540) preached Sunday November 15th 1863 at the Metropolitan Tabernacle. 'He shall gather the lambs with his arm, and carry them in his bosom.' *(Isaiah 40.11)*

world to be changed to her. She now loves alone the best things, and wishes in future by God's grace to live wholly for Jesus. She wishes to be baptised out of love to Jesus and obedience to his command.

I feel this to be a truly genuine case of conversion. She is an intelligent, thoughtful girl, able well to give a reason for the hope that is in her.

Gave a card. *William Olney*

There is a book in the Tabernacle archives with photographs of 100 of the members who voluntecred as Sunday School teachers during the early part of Spurgeon's pastorate. By the end of his ministry there were 27 Sunday and Ragged Schools ministering to 8,000 children with 600 teachers, not to mention numerous young adult Bible classes.

Jane Maria Riley
42 Penton Place,
Walworth

IN the Sabbath School in Mrs Bigg's class, and so frequently heard Mr Spurgeon. Was first impressed under the sermon, 'Whereas I was blind now I see.' This convinced her of sin but she did not find peace for some time. She prayed earnestly for forgiveness for many weeks, and at last about ten months ago, whilst crying to God in prayer on her bed in the night-time, she felt the blood of Jesus applied to her conscience, and she was able to trust fully to him. She then found joy

'Simple But Sound'
(2955) preached in the year 1863 at the Metropolitan Tabernacle. 'One thing I know, that, whereas I was blind, now I see.' *(John 9.25)*

and peace in believing. Since that time she has had a steady confidence in the Saviour and rejoices fully in him. Wishes to be baptised out of love to Jesus and obedience to his command.

She is very much tried at home with an ungodly father and mother, especially her father who opposes her continually, and has threatened to turn her out of doors if she is baptised. She still, however, wishes to come, and having given me clear evidence of the work of grace in her heart, gave a card. *William Olney*

Maryanne Jane Alley
2 Nottingham Place,
South Street, Walworth
Age: 16

IN Miss Stephen's class in Sabbath School. Was first led to Christ by Mr Spurgeon speaking against a form of prayer. She then gave up saying prayers and began to pray. She sought forgiveness continually and a new heart, but did not find the Saviour till the third of November last when at a prayer meeting with her teachers. She was led to look to Jesus and is now trusting in him alone. She finds prayer a privilege, and the Bible a pleasure to read. She now loves the things and persons she did not once, and hates those she once loved. She wishes to be baptised out of love to Christ and obedience to his command. *William Olney*

George Henry Middleton
46 Carter Street, Walworth
Lodges at 34 Clerkenwell

ABOUT two and a half years ago was deeply convinced of sin under the preaching of Mr Hugh Allen. He had experienced some workings in his conscience before this when engaged in a seafaring life, but the effectual work does not seem to have commenced till the time stated above. He was some months in trouble of soul, but the ministry of Mr Hugh Allen seemed to give him some peace of soul. But it was not steadfast. And it was not till about six months ago while attending the prayer meeting at Crosby Hall, that he received full assurance of faith, and ever since then he has been able to rejoice in a finished salvation.

He believes that he was too much addicted to looking at self, and that kept him in darkness of soul. But the clear way in which Christ had been set before him by our pastor and also by the prayers of the brethren at Crosby Hall, he has been led by the Spirit to see *Jesus only* as his Saviour. He has also come to see baptism as plainly a command of Christ and wishes to walk in accordance thereto. He is full of gratitude at looking back upon his life, and seeing how the Lord was working with him and watching over him, while in his dangerous occupation at sea. He is amazed at the change which has been wrought in him, never feeling so happy as when in the house of God, and engaged in his worship and service.

I had a long conversation with this brother and was much pleased with him. He feels more than he can find words to express, and I believe has a good notion of the doctrines of grace. In his own words – 'I am very illiterate, but I have got it *here*' (in his heart). I gave him a card. *Frederick Grose*

I cannot see this case very clearly, but I have hoped for the best. His story is a terrible muddle. It may be a skein of silk but I cannot unwind it. I trust the messenger *[the elder or deacon appointed to visit]* will be very particular. He is out of situation and ought to get one. *CHS*

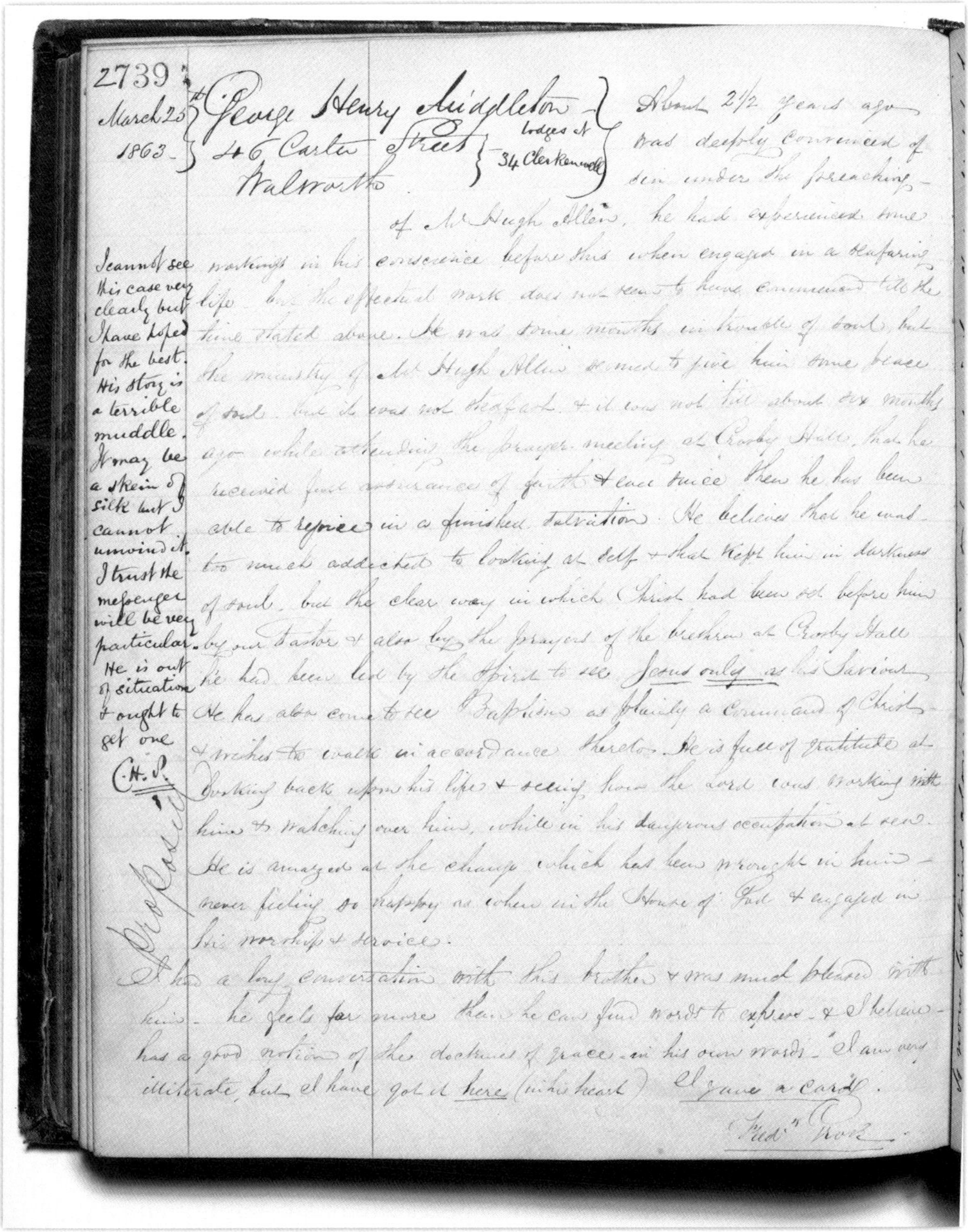

2739

March 25 1863 — George Henry Middleton ? 46 Carter Street Walworth. lodges at 34 Clerkenwell

About 2½ years ago was deeply convinced of sin under the preaching — of Mr Hugh Allen. He had experienced some workings in his conscience before this when engaged in a seafaring life but the effectual work does not seem to have commenced till the time stated above. He was some months in trouble of soul, but the ministry of Mr Hugh Allen seemed to give him some peace of soul but he was not steadfast. & it was not till about six months ago while attending the prayer meeting at Crosby Hall, that he received full assurances of faith & once since then he has been able to rejoice in a finished salvation. He believes that he was too much addicted to looking at self & that kept him in darkness of soul, but the clear way in which Christ had been set before him by our Pastor & also by the prayers of the brethren at Crosby Hall he had been led by the Spirit to see Jesus only as his Saviour. He has also come to see Baptism as plainly a command of Christ & wishes to walk in accordance thereto. He is full of gratitude at looking back upon his life & seeing how the Lord was working with him & watching over him, while in his dangerous occupation at sea. He is amazed at the change which has been wrought in him — never feeling so happy as when in the House of God & engaged in his worship & service.

I had a long conversation with this brother & was much pleased with him. He feels far more than he can find words to express. & I believe has a good notion of the doctrines of grace — in his own words "I am very illiterate, but I have got it here" (in his heart). I gave a card.

Fred. Grose

Margin note (left):
I cannot see his case very clearly but I have hoped for the best. His story is a terrible muddle. It may be a skein of silk but I cannot unwind it. I trust the messenger will be very particular. He is out of situation & ought to get one.

C.H.S.

Pro: Comfort

Feby 25 1863

2736

James Hazell
38 Minto Street
Long Lane
Bermondsey

Abt 4 y[ea]rs Since it pleased God to afflict him — at which time he was the subject of deep convictions his past life of sin & wickedness was all brought before him — he felt he was going to Hell as fast as he could — but he got better & at that time he went into the country to see his Father who was a wicked profligate man & he told him in a very careless manner that a member of Mr Spurgeons (Mr Bourne) had invited him to go to Exeter Hall to hear Mr S — & the answer his father made very much struck him — "I would go if I were you I would take that mans advice" — when he came home he went & some remarks in the Sermon struck him very much in allusion to the Sabbath it was like a ladder the spaces were the weeks, & the rounds were the Sabbaths & thus we get a Sabbath nearer Heaven, after that he went to hear Mr Carter at the Surrey Theatre. & the sermon was on the Sufferings & Crucifixion of Christ the Crown of Thorns. he then obtained a sight of Christ as suffering for Sin — & such a sight he has never lost — & has since follow Christ & walks by faith & would wish to join a Christian Church sees Baptism to be a Command & is anxious to obey it   was well satisfied with him & gave him a Card is known to Bro Bowles & others

John Ward

Cabinet maker in Clerkenwell
works at Mr Bourne, 2 St Warner Street

Reduced-size photograph of testimony to the right written out by elder John
Ward (see page 135 for information about Mr Ward).
(The size of the original books is 21cm wide by 25 cm tall.)

> **James Hazell**
> 34 Mint Street,
> Long Lane, Bermondsey

ABOUT four years since it pleased God to afflict him, at which time he was the subject of deep convictions. His past life of sin and wickedness was all brought before him, and he felt he was going to hell as fast as he could. But he got better, and about that time he went into the country to see his father, who was a wicked, profligate man. And he told him, in a very careless manner, that a member of Mr Spurgeon's (Mr Bourne) had invited him to go to Exeter Hall to hear Mr S. And the answer his father made very much struck him – 'I would go if I were you. I would take that man's advice.'

When he came home, he went, and some remarks in the sermon struck him very much – viz. in allusion to the Sabbath. It was like a ladder – the spaces were the weeks, and the rounds were the Sabbaths, and thus we get a Sabbath nearer Heaven. After that he went to hear Mr Carter at the Surrey Theatre, and the sermon was

Elephant & Castle, 1860
(Courtesy: London Metropolitan Archives, City of London)

on the sufferings and crucifixion of Christ – the crown of thorns. He then obtained a sight of Christ as suffering for sin. And such a sight he has never lost, and has since followed Christ, and walks by faith, and would wish to join a Christian church. Sees baptism to be a command and is anxious to obey it. Was well satisfied with him and gave him a card. Is known to Brother Bowles and others.

John Ward

Cabinet maker in Clerkenwell, works at Mr Bourne, 2 Gt Warner Street. To call and see the wife, and also to Mr Bourne.

Mary Ann Longbottom
3 Berkley Terrace, Kennington Park

ONE who can talk rather fast, and has a very good opinion of herself – I think too much so to join this church. *J W Brown*

Henry Bradford
36 Gutter Lane, Cheapside (at Messrs W & R Morely)

DID not know the Lord till he came to the Tabernacle, which was last March. Was first brought by G Blay. Curiosity was the first impulse, and after that he had a desire to come, he could not keep away. The first teaching he got was to undo all that he had ever done and thought before, and was made very unhappy. That made him cry to the Lord, but believes he prayed too much in his own strength, but found he must go deeper than that. He was taught there was only one way. The sermon 'This is his commandment that ye believe &c' brought his soul to Christ, and as a great sinner to cast himself wholly on him for mercy and salvation.

'The Warrant of Faith'
(531) preached Sunday September 20th 1863 at the Metropolitan Tabernacle. 'And this is his commandment, That we should believe on the name of his Son Jesus Christ.' *(1 John 3.23)*

While he daily feels and mourns over imperfections which constantly mingle with all that he does, he knows they are all atoned for. And the efficacy of the Saviour's

INTERVIEWING ELDERS

John Ward

Spurgeon expressed appreciation of John Ward in the 1890 *The Sword and the Trowel*: 'He joined the church by baptism in October 1835, and consequently has been in its membership for nearly 55 years, and is the first male member now upon the church-roll. He was among the first brethren who were elected to the office of elder when the church was led to see that the two offices of deacon and elder were needful to a scriptural church. This was on January 12th 1859. Of the nine then chosen, he is the only one who continues in the office. Few men attain the age of 85, and yet retain so much clearness of mind and comparative vigour of body. When seen walking to and from the house of God, one would think him far younger. Mr Ward had no desire to be seen in our pages; for he has been a quiet and retiring helper of the work; but his name has appeared in almost all important documents recording our church history, from the fact of his being the senior elder; and for that reason we felt that he must be placed in this "magazine of memorial," for many would naturally inquire, "Who is John Ward?" He has seen the church in prosperity and in adversity; he stuck to her gates when she was minished and brought low, and as a reward he sees a blessing upon his family, of whom the most are followers of the Lord.'

sacrifice is in being the Son of God made flesh, taking on him our nature, and that he has a personal interest in his death as no one else can save him.

This I believe to be an excellent case and very clear, and gave him a card.

John Ward

From the book *Street Life in London* by John Thomson, published in 1876. The chapter – 'Flooding in Lambeth' describes the sufferings of the poor in Lambeth caused by the annual tidal overflow of the Thames. Many people had chronic illnesses from living in damp, crowded houses. The woman in the centre worked at home making lace, both she and the children suffering from damp-related health problems. Her husband worked from 4am-8pm, and 6am-6pm Sundays, as a horse-keeper, earning 25 shillings a week.

Spurgeon said that the Tabernacle congregation always had a larger proportion of poorer people. (Courtesy: LSE Library)

Henry Chinnery
81 Great Guildford Street

THIS good brother has been long hesitating about joining the church, having got it into his head that a certain degree of perfection, if not perfection itself, was necessary. He has been trying to work himself up to that, but all his efforts failing. And having like the poor debtors nothing to pay, he has come at last just as he is, 'a poor sinner and nothing at all', finding that Jesus Christ is his 'all in all'. He came first to New Park Street when the pastor preached at Exeter Hall, and seemed so led that, although tempted over and over again not to come, insomuch that he often came when the service had begun some quarter or half an hour, yet he seemed as though he could not keep away, though at the same time he had to suffer many sneers and jeers even then. Some few months after he first attended, he was convinced of sin under one of those who then occasionally preached. It seemed to him that someone had told the minister all that he had ever done. This drove him to prayer. By degrees light broke in upon his soul, and he feels confident that '*Jesus had found him and will not leave him.*' These are his own words.

Our good brother I have long noticed very regular in attendance upon the means of grace, and is in good reputation at New Park Street. Mr Collins, I know, thought well of him and Mr Burton and myself, and therefore recommend him.

Frederick Grose

> **Humphrey White**
> 21 West Street, Walworth
> Age: 23

IS son to our esteemed brother and sister of the same name. Used to frequent tea gardens and such like places of amusement, and plunged into the very depths of sin. His father used to pray with and for him, and when once asked upstairs to a prayer meeting, he at first refused but eventually went, but only to please his father. Used occasionally to come to Mr Hanks' class, and about three weeks ago while his father and a good Christian brother, a soldier of the name of Broom, were praying, he felt deeply affected and felt greatly his burden of sin. This led him to pray *himself* secretly in the meeting. And Mr Spurgeon the same evening preached from the words 'Escape for thy life.' He describes his feelings as being wretched and yet joyful – wretched on account of sin, but joyful that there

**'The Ship on Fire –
A Voice of Warning'**
(550) preached on Sunday November 8th 1863. 'Thou hast magnified thy mercy, which thou hast shewed unto me in saving my life.' *(Genesis 19.19)*

November 1863 saw the ship *Amazon* catch fire and sink whilst moored off Broadstairs. All passengers and crew were rescued. Spurgeon said: 'Now, as the good brother who was captain to that vessel constantly comes here when he is on shore, and as he is sitting in the midst of you tonight, I thought I might use the burning of this vessel as a picture of spiritual things, out of which I might make an illustrated sermon. These things happen not without design, and should not escape without improvement.'

was a hope set before him in the Gospel. He feels confident that he is a changed character, that he never can go back to his old ways now. His whole trust is in Christ. Last Sunday he felt especially blest while in the class. Wishes to be baptised in obedience to Christ's command.

I believe this young man to be a sincere believer. His father and mother both bear testimony to the changes that have been wrought in him, I therefore gave him a card. *Frederick Grose*

> **Catherine Flint**
> 47 Whenlock Street,
> New North Road

THIS sister is locked up in 'Doubting Castle' and has been so for eight years, during which time she has attended the ministry of our pastor. She has a deep conviction of her own sinfulness and that Christ died for sinners, but did he die for her? That is the unsettled point.

I hardly know what to do with this case and asked Brother Cook to see her. I quite believe with him that she is a child of God though very much harassed by the enemy, and gave her a card.

William Bowker

> **James Endersley**
> 6 Little Pleasant Row,
> East Lane, Walworth

A TAILOR working for a whole-sale house in the City. Last July in walking along the Walworth Road in a weekday evening, he heard a young man preaching on 'the coming of the Lord draweth nigh'. He was then aroused to a sense of his danger and led to cry for mercy and forgiveness. His convictions of sin have been very deep and he was some months finding peace. That came at last under a sermon from our dear pastor, 'If we sin we have an advocate with the Father, even Jesus Christ the righteous.'

'The Sinner's Advocate' (515) preached Sunday June 21st 1863 at the Metropolitan Tabernacle. 'My little children, these things write I unto you, that ye sin not. And if any man sin, we have an advocate with the Father, Jesus Christ the righteous.' *(1 John 2.1)*

This gave him peace. He then saw the work of the Saviour as his substitute and was led to rest wholly on the blood and righteousness of the Saviour. He now very often weeps to the praise of the grace and goodness he has found. He has no other, and wants no other hope for salvation and eternal life but Jesus. He wishes to be baptised and join the church out of love to Christ and obedience to his command. Gave a card with pleasure.

William Olney

> **Selina Clarke**
> 12 South Villa, Clapham Rd

THIS young woman, although brought up in the Sabbath School, has gone into the world and its pleasures even as she could. But through a friend with whom she works, was induced to come and hear our pastor. This was two years ago. Went again into the world attending theatre, balls, concert rooms, and got acquainted with Humphrey White *[see testimony on page 137]*, now a member with us, but then going to those places of amusement. Was led by our brother to attend regularly the means of grace at the Tabernacle, when it pleased God to meet with her. The sermon on the second Sabbath in this year, with a prayer meeting which our Brother White held when they reached home was, she believes, blessed to her conversion. Has attended Mrs Bartlett's class for about a year on and off, but regularly for this last three months. This is a most remarkable instance of divine grace. Our sister White has been made a good blessing to her.

I have great pleasure in giving her a card. *George Croker*

> **John Lee**
> 25 Edward Street,
> Dockhead, Bermondsey

THIS lad attended the meetings held at Dockhead where some of the students from the Tabernacle preached. About eight months since was deeply impressed with the conversation a Christian man had with some other lads, but this wore off and he went again into the world. But

Extract from Church Meeting book, 1861: There are several very wonderful cases among those above in which sin has abounded, and the grace of God has superabounded. The two marked X were harlots, may they be Rahabs. The brother marked ·//· was a very violent infidel, but by the Holy Ghost has received the faith of God's elect. The Lord be praised. CHS

conscience was not asleep, and he went back to the School, and from that time he has been enabled to enjoy peace.

I had a very lengthened conversation with him, and took particular pains to ascertain whether the work of grace had begun, but from his simple answers to my questions I was led to the conclusion that he is a partaker of saving grace. He is but a babe indeed but I believe there is life. Mr Butler, the superintendent of the School (and a member with us), and Miss Figgs have had conversation with him and recommend him to us.

Gave a card. *G Croker*

> **Benjamin Froud**
> 34 Warner Street,
> Dover Road

LIVES with Mrs Christy and Co, hatters* at Bermondsey. Mr Oxford and Mr Taylor, members with us, live in the same employ. Through the blessing of the Holy Spirit upon their instruction and warnings, this

---

* Christy's Hats is still in existence, founded by William Miller Christy, an English Quaker.

youth has been seriously impressed and awakened to a sense of his state as a lost sinner. He professes that he has obtained pardon and peace in believing on Christ. Also that it is his constant prayer to be taught and sanctified by the Spirit, and enabled early and for ever to consecrate his life to Christ and his church. Although young, and as yet but partially informed in the things of God, I believe the root of the matter is in him and that he has spiritual life in him.

Has attended our pastor's ministry with profit for about eight months, and is at as many weekday evening meetings as possible.

Gave a card.

John T Olney

> **Rachel Williams**
> 7 Bermondsey Square,
> Bermondsey

FIRST brought here by our sister Banks, but heard Mr Spurgeon at Maze Pond Chapel and received impressions then. From the moment she heard his voice she again felt the old impressions renewed. After attending here some time, she became so alarmed at her state as a sinner that she was constrained to cry for mercy. And this continued all one night, bathing her pillow with tears and thus she fell asleep. When she awoke, she felt much happier and could sing hymns of joy. Never felt so happy before and has been happy ever since. Her husband knows she is happy, her neighbours know she is happy, everybody knows she is happy, and she knows she is happy, and I believe she is happy.

Gave her a card.

J Cooper

'Wherefore seeing we also are compassed about
with so great a cloud of witnesses, let us lay aside every weight,
and the sin which doth so easily beset us, and let us run with
patience the race that is set before us, looking unto Jesus
the author and finisher of our faith.'
(Hebrews 12.1-2)

www.MetropolitanTabernacle.org

The Metropolitan Tabernacle is still a large congregation
in central London proclaiming the Gospel of salvation
and the doctrines of grace.

See web site for details of services, *Sword & Trowel*
magazine, Seminary, many other ministries, and free
sermon downloads.

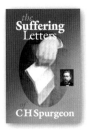

The Suffering Letters
of C H Spurgeon

155 pages, illustrated paperback, ISBN 978 1 870855 60 0

These remarkable letters, written from a suffering pastor to his congregation, abound in exhortations to godliness, zeal and prayer. They provide a unique insight into Spurgeon's life, and into the fervent soul-winning activity which was, alongside the preaching, a leading feature of an historic Calvinistic church.

Notes on Spurgeon's ministry set the letters in context, and several classic sermonettes written during sickness are included, along with 16 pages of colour pictures of original letters.

Classic Counsels
of C H Spurgeon

126 pages, paperback, ISBN 978 1 870855 42 6

A selection of edited messages suitable for our time. Some were originally given to the Tabernacle Prayer Meeting, and are missed by other selections of Spurgeon sermons.

Topics included are: obtaining certain assurance; help for doubting seekers; encouraging outsiders and advising seekers; relief for the downcast; developing faith; the Christian and places of entertainment; and others.

The Personal Spiritual Life
Peter Masters

139 pages, paperback, ISBN 978 1 870855 50 1

From the personal indwelling of the Holy Spirit to living a life of commitment these chapters stir and encourage readers to advance spiritually.

In what sense may we 'feel' the presence of the Lord? What was the apostle Paul's method for progress in holiness? How may we identify our spiritual gifts? And how may we count more for the Lord, and sustain spiritual joy? These are among the themes of this tonic for present-day disciples of Christ.

www.wakemantrust.org